My Best Advice

My Best Advice

PROVEN RULES FOR EFFECTIVE LEADERSHIP

Tim Rahschulte, Ryan Halley, and Russ Martinelli

Published by IntelliPress Media.

Library of Congress Cataloging-in-Publication Data is Available

ISBN-13: 9780999589403 (paperback publication)
ISBN-13: 978-0-9995894-1-0 (e-book publication)

ISBN-10: 0999589407
Library of Congress Control Number: 2017917015
IntelliPress Media, LLC, PORTLAND, OR

Cover Design: IntelliPress Media

Contents

Acknowledgments

We would like to thank the many leaders we've learned from over the years, especially those we've had the privilege to meet in person, discuss leadership best practices with, and come to call friends. We're truly blessed to have such a wonderful community of people in our lives. While we can never repay you for the time, wisdom, guidance, insights, and perspective you've provided us, we'll do our absolute best to pay it forward and pass it on—just as you have done for us.

Thank you.

Introduction

L eadership. Just reading the word *leadership* likely creates in your mind an image of someone who has inspired you, challenged you, encouraged you, and helped you to believe in yourself. It's likely to be someone you admire. Who's that person? Whom do you look up to? Who's your leader icon, mentor, or idol? Whom do you go to for advice, guidance, and direction?

Whoever comes to mind right now has something in common with all other great leaders. They all have guiding advice based on their experiences. You may call them laws, mantras, maxims, axioms, or aphorisms. We call them *rules*.

It doesn't matter if the leader you have in mind is a sports star, business mogul, executive coach, Hollywood actress, political powerhouse, high school teacher, friend, parent, sibling, or anyone else for that matter. This person's leadership know-how is often readily available and willingly provided in small bursts of wisdom, learned over time and proven true by experience. That's what *My Best Advice* is: a set of lessons learned and best practices that serve as reminders for us about what to do, how to do it, and why to do it at all as we go about our lives and careers. We say lives *and* careers because these rules are as applicable in the home as they are in the office, useful in the family room and the boardroom, and equally valuable in any residential community or business environment.

Now you may not like the word *rules*. Possibly your mind immediately thinks of something rigid, such as a mandate that must be followed at all costs. Or worse yet, maybe you're thinking about the kinds of rules others force upon you along with monitoring to ensure your compliance. These can be helpful in some situations, but they're not the kind of rules we're talking about here. The rules we'll be detailing are motivating and inspiring. They call us to live the kind of life that's only possible with a deep sense of understanding and appreciation, followed by deliberate action. These are rules that help to provide perspective, insights, and ways forward when addressing perhaps the two most important questions we should be asking ourselves every day:

1. What will I do with the world as I find it?
2. What shows up when I do?

Think about these questions. They may be curious questions, or you may have started to think of a response for each of them already. The real value in the "answer" to each question, however, is in discovering how you'll align your actions with intended outcomes so that reality plays out the way that you desire. As we learned from Marc Varner, the chief information security officer at YUM! Brands, "Bad days will come that will put you under pressure and you may not act the way you would want to act." In other words, showing up in the manner that you expect requires a level of forethought and intentionality that doesn't happen without some careful attention, reflection, and preparation. Being a great leader requires situational understanding and deliberate action about what you'll do with the world as you find it, which will be contingent upon what shows up when you do.

Over the last several years, we've conducted thousands of interviews and met directly with hundreds of truly exceptional leaders. Some are industry executives, others are coaches, some are in government roles, and others are world-renowned academics. In the process of meeting, working with, and learning from these leaders, we've captured their leadership advice, lessons they've learned, and rules they follow that have helped enable their success. Understanding, learning, and applying leadership rules have made these leaders, their teams, their organizations, and the communities in which they participate better. Each of these leaders passes his or her rules on to help develop other leaders and enable their success, which similarly cascades to their teams, organizations, and communities. These leaders' rules capture the essence of the various ways in which we desire to show up and contribute to the world—however we may find it.

Whether you're considering personal or professional aspects of your life, you'll find the effectiveness of these rules to be internally driven. They're not forced upon you from the outside; rather, they're constructed, embraced, and followed because you determine that they're important. Actually, that's part of the difficulty with the kind of rules that we're talking about—they are what you make of them and will rarely be lived out unless you own the process of doing so. It's a process of awareness and continual improvement—understanding, applying, reflecting, adapting, and passing on your own knowledge and rules through your actions and behaviors.

The leadership rules presented here represent aspirational ideas, action targets, or aiming points. However you want to view and use them, these rules point to the kinds of actions and behavior you want to exhibit when and where you show up. The power of leadership rules like these is that they guide us closer and closer to the intended mark we aim for, with the intent of continually increasing our awareness and improvement over time and with more experience. If you've ever gone bowling, you understand this concept. Remember those bumpers placed in the gutters to prevent a wayward ball from going off the lane? The ball we roll when and where we show up may not turn out to be a strike, but the bumpers ensure that the outcome is more closely aligned with what we hoped for than would've been the case without them. When enacted, leadership rules work like those bowling bumpers. They don't ensure that we hit the target with our actions every time, but they do keep us within a set of boundaries and point us closer to where we want to be and the leaders we want to become.

So what will you do with the world as you find it? What will show up when you do? Allow the wisdom contained in the following pages, and your own rules created from your experience with *My Best Advice*, to move you closer to living your responses with greater alignment to your desired leadership style. Doing so will make you better and, as a result, will make your teams, company, family, and community better as well.

User Guide (Don't Just Read It—*Use* It!)

Not often is there a user guide to accompany a book. After all, books are rather straightforward: open the cover, read, turn the page, read, turn the page, read, turn the page…and repeat until done. You know how a book works. But make no mistake: what you're reading isn't just a book; it's a *workbook*. There's a sizable difference between the two. While we're confident that you'll find the content in this workbook to be interesting, entertaining, and of practical value, our real intent is that you'll invest time not just to read it but also to write in it, highlight passages throughout it, spill coffee on it, talk about it with colleagues, flag important pages, and review it regularly for perspective, direction, and inspiration. We hope that years from now, it's ragged from use but still providing as much value and comfort as it did when it was new.

The work you put into this workbook can easily transform it into your journal of exceptional leadership insights and rules. It can become a leadership manual from which you learn and establish your leadership style and, in turn, mentor others to be their absolute best. So you see, it's not meant to simply be read; it's meant to be studied. It's meant to make existing leaders better and aspiring leaders ready. It's meant to facilitate a journey of self-development, learning, and growth. To help you facilitate development, learning, and growth, there are two analogies throughout this workbook: one is to help with the development of your leadership style, and it focuses on a physical structure like a high-rise building relative to thinking about you as a leader and how to develop your leadership style, and the other is to help you understand that leadership is a process or an ongoing journey.

Have you ever taken the Amtrak train from Seattle to Chicago? That's a journey. It'll take you nearly sixty-five hours to make that trip. Once you catch the train at the Station Building on South Jackson Street in Seattle, you'll stop at forty stations along your route to Chicago.

Why do we bring this up? Well, while you could probably skim through this workbook in sixty-five minutes, why not take sixty-five hours instead? Sure, there are faster and more direct routes than Amtrak's to get from Seattle to Chicago, and it certainly would be a faster and a more direct route to read *My Best Advice* cover to cover in isolation. However, leaders get better by reflecting, sharing, practicing, and learning with their teams and other leaders. We learned the importance of this from Harry Kraemer, the former chief executive officer and chairman of Baxter International, now clinical professor of strategy at Northwestern University's Kellogg School of Management, and author of *From Values to Action*. He said, "If I'm not self-reflective, can I really know myself? If I don't know myself, can I really lead myself? If I can't lead myself, can I really lead others?" The answer to each question is no.

So rather than shortcutting your journey, and instead of putting your head down for the sixty-five hours and forty stops on the train to simply get through it, pull back every now and then to pause, reflect, and talk with your friends, colleagues, and other leaders about where you are and where you're going. Instead of treating each stop like an inconvenient obstacle, adopt the mindset that each stop presents an opportunity for engagement with others, self-reflection, learning, and growth. In other words, take a break on occasion to talk about what you're seeing in the world and what you're going to do with the world as you find it.

You'll find that the end of each section of this workbook serves as an intentional guidepost on your journey. While there are questions to consider within many of the rules, as well as at the end of each chapter, there are also questions at the end of each section, which are meant to remind you to pause and reflect. For example, by the time you finish studying the fourteen rules in section 1 regarding mindset, purpose, and perspective, you're likely to find yourself beyond the far eastern border of Washington State and the Spokane station, your sixth stop in the journey to Chicago. Take time thereabouts to think about the foundation of your leadership. By the time you get to the halfway point, you'll be rolling into Williston, North Dakota, the twentieth station. Around that point, stop reading to reflect on the seventeen rules in section 2 regarding vision, preparation, and action, which comprise the three pillars that rise up from the foundation of all truly exceptional leaders. At the thirty-third station, you'll find yourself in LaCrosse, Wisconsin. By that station, or somewhere nearby, you'll certainly want to think deeply about people leadership, team leadership, and self-leadership and the eighteen rules in that section. Your fortieth station is your destination on this journey: Chicago. It's there that you'll want to reflect on the importance of learning and the five rules within that section.

As you read *My Best Advice*, you'll find leadership to be a process, and you'll realize it's a learning journey as much as anything else. You'll never really "arrive" when it comes to leadership, but when in Chicago, if you've embraced the rules in this workbook and committed to continuous improvement toward being a truly exceptional leader, we suspect that you'll leave the train, walk out of the station, pause, reflect, and say, "Wow! What a ride."

The time you invest to know who you are and the leader you aim to be will prove important when it comes to thinking and knowing what shows up when you do and will inform your actions regarding what you will do with the world as you find it. Spend the time necessary to be the leader you aspire to be.

Enjoy the journey!

Section 1
The Foundation of Great Leaders and Leadership

The strength and efficacy of anything is based on the foundation upon which it's built. This is true for physical structures, such as high-rise buildings, and nonphysical structures, such as the culture of a high-performing team and the accomplishments the members of that team can achieve together. It's also true for leaders and leadership.

This first section of *My Best Advice* contains fourteen rules. Each rule is important on its own, but together they serve as the foundation for what makes great leaders great and their leadership truly exceptional. These fourteen rules describe the power of *mindset,* the importance of *purpose,* and the significance of *perspective.*

Mindset
Rule 1.	The foundation of success is a positive mindset.
Rule 2.	You're right about your belief in yourself.
Rule 3.	Don't confuse self-doubt with someone else's insecurity.
Rule 4.	You may not get the chance to do a better job tomorrow.

Purpose
Rule 5.	Don't forget why you do what you do.
Rule 6.	If you don't care, no one else will either.
Rule 7.	Know what you're willing to give.
Rule 8.	The purpose of business is people serving people.
Rule 9.	The purpose of people is finding meaning in work.
Rule 10.	Leadership is art, and you sign your name to it every day.

Perspective
Rule 11.	Your perspective may be yours alone.
Rule 12.	Have a point of view, but be willing to change it.
Rule 13.	Stop believing everything you think.
Rule 14.	No one has all the answers all the time.

Your ability to accomplish anything starts with what you believe is possible. If you don't believe you can accomplish your goals, you put yourself and those you lead at a mental and philosophical deficit that's hard to overcome. If, however, you believe in your opportunity to succeed, you immediately increase the likelihood that you will. It's a mindset. It's an attitude. It's an outlook you hold about yourself and others that becomes the lens through which you can picture what's possible. It's so important we made it the first rule: *the foundation of success is a positive mindset.*

The way you think matters because it drives the way you act; in turn, the way you act reinforces the way you think. So the way you think is crucial. However, mindset alone, regardless how positive, won't ensure that your vision of what's possible will indeed become reality; other variables also need to be in place for you to achieve your goals. Whatever the goal, you'll need at least some ambition, skill, foresight, probably a dose of good luck, ample humility to learn along the way, sustained perseverance, and a team connected to a purpose.

Truly exceptional leaders know that the underlying purpose of any organizational success, team accomplishment, or personal milestone is about people—both the ones who benefit from whatever you create or accomplish and those on your team who work together to make it happen. Connecting your team to a purpose requires sharing the picture of what you see as possible and enabling the team to see its importance as clearly as you do. This is about creating alignment of purpose and a human connection to the collaboration necessary to achieve that purpose.

It's one thing to be able to envision the importance of an accomplishment, but it's something entirely different, something much more meaningful, to effectively express the purpose of your work and effort. Doing so will provide the reason for others to engage, because it rationalizes and emotionalizes the work and effort needed relative to the accomplishment.

People, especially those on your team, won't commit or care about what you can see as possible until they know how much you care about the *purpose* of what's possible and their role in helping to achieve it. This is the foundation of accomplishing anything great. When a positive mindset is coupled with a well-defined purpose, a leader finds care and commitment. This care and commitment isn't reserved for the leader alone; rather, it's found among the entire team because of the team members' connection to one another through their common purpose. Leveraging that with intentional behavior and action enables you to realize a mindset of what's possible.

It's important to know, however, that your mindset and purpose are not universal. The things that motivate you won't necessarily motivate everyone. It's for this reason that we must understand perspective. We each have perspective: a point of view of things currently happening around us and of what's possible because of us. It's our sense of things. In some cases, we find that our perspective is directly aligned with others'. In other cases, however, individual perspectives are quite different. The best leaders work continually to ensure integration of the team's perspectives, strengthen the care and commitment the team members have for one another, and maintain belief individually and collectively in their ability to achieve the common purpose that their mindset pictures as possible.

As you prepare to read section 1, pause for a moment to think about your role as a leader. Perhaps you're already an effective leader but are looking to get better. Or maybe you're entering a new leadership position and want to learn what it takes to be most effective. Or you may be aspiring to a leadership role and are looking to learn what separates the best leaders from everyone else. All are great reasons to keep reading and studying. This section details the power of *mindset*, the importance of *purpose*, and the significance of *perspective*, which together contain the rules that, when enacted, galvanize the foundation of truly exceptional leaders. Consider each rule carefully, mark those you want to adopt as your own, share your new lessons and key takeaways with others, and document your own rules that, when put into practice, will make you even more effective.

Mindset

Rule 1. The foundation of success is a positive mindset.

N othing is achieved without a belief that it can be done. That's a mindset. Mindset is an attitude that colors our view of the world and what's possible in—and beyond—it. Mindset is the initiating force behind Elon Musk's goal to colonize Mars. Similarly, mindset is the initiating force anyone leverages to build something new, reengineer something to be better, or to bring about a change in things. Regardless of whether that change is incremental and evolutionary or transformational and revolutionary, achieving it starts with a positive mindset.

Our mindset initiates a sense of possibility from which our behavior and actions follow. Therefore, our mindset serves as the foundation of our results. Those most successful have an unwaveringly positive mindset about who they are and the impact they'll have.

While all this may seem rather obvious, there's something else important about our mindset: it has a multiplying effect on those around us. It scales and reaches beyond oneself.

The greatest leaders know the power of mindset. This remarkable power is one reason Colin Powell, arguably one of the greatest leaders in US military history, who retired as a four-star army general, served as secretary of state, led the military of the United

States while serving as the chairman of the joint chiefs, and authored the book *It Worked for Me: In Life and Leadership*, often shares this critical piece of leadership advice: "Perpetual optimism is a force multiplier." Now, to be sure, the opposite is also true.

Whether negative or positive, your mindset multiplies as it affects those around you. It's for this reason that Ashley Ferguson, the global director of strategy, governance, risk, and compliance at SecureWorks, coaches her employees and believes in the need for leaders to "be positive, be open, be truthful, and stay optimistic." She emphasizes this because she knows that attitude is contagious, especially if you're in a leadership role.

If you're wondering if you're a leader, know that we're all leaders some of the time and followers all of the time. So yes, you're a leader, and therefore your attitude is quite important.

Regardless of role, title, or rank, make the choice to be positive. Have an "it can be done" attitude, which just happens to be another piece of leadership advice from Colin Powell. This positivity is necessary because the root cause of your results is attitude, and the foundation of your success is a positive mindset.

Rule 2. You're right about your belief in yourself.

You may think the idea of mindset, as noted in rule 1, is too "soft" to spend much time on these days. Well, think about your mindset for a moment. Are you perpetually optimistic or routinely pessimistic? Do you dream big from a perspective of abundance or think small from a point of scarcity? Do you have a general philosophy of "it can be done," or do you immediately focus on why things can't be done?

There's no right or wrong in your thinking, but it's true that you're right about your belief in yourself. You're right about what you believe is possible and impossible. That's mindset. It's also self-efficacy, and it plays an important role in how you show up and how you think about goals (especially big ones), challenges, engagement, teamwork, and your daily routines. Remember when we asked what shows up when you do? Well, the answer really depends on your mindset and your belief in yourself. If you believe you can't, you won't. If you believe you can, then you can.

Consider the power of self-efficacy when thinking about yourself. We've all read or heard stories about someone who accomplished something amazing, something that seemed impossible to even think about, let alone achieve. As those stories often go, when the achiever of such a feat is asked how he or she accomplished it, the reply is something like, "Well, no one ever told me I *couldn't* do it, so I just did it."

Unfortunately, these stories don't happen nearly as often as they should. Far too many people are programmed to work and live and dream and hope within constraints, with a scarcity mindset, rather than recognizing limitless opportunities from leveraging an abundance mindset. This is unfortunate because constraints lead to conformity, which leads to status quo, which leads to mediocrity, which breeds cynics, skeptics, and doubters. It's a downward spiral.

You don't have to look very hard to find cynicism these days. In a time when we need more perpetual optimism and hope, it seems the supply of cynicism is overwhelming the demand for positivity, and this pervasive negativity affects everything and everyone it touches, thereby fueling the negativity spiral.

Fortunately, the opposite is also true. Positive individuals, teams, organizations, and communities overcome negativity and make the choice to demonstrate a source of relentless optimism and an attitude of continual opportunity alongside the expectation of achieving excellence. That's the positive mindset of optimistic people and exceptional leaders.

Optimistic people believe that they will succeed, that they can be great, and that they can win. Your success will start the same way it starts for anyone: with a belief that it's possible. Power and momentum are achieved when a positive mindset meets with a positive belief in yourself.

Henry Ford once said, "Whether you think you can or think you can't, you're right." Don't underestimate yourself and your ability to positively affect your environment. People do it every day. You can, too. Having a positive mindset is a choice. It's a choice to focus on the future rather than dwelling on the past, on action without being mired in analysis, on possibility and opportunity rather than issues and problems, and to focus on creating options and solutions without ever accepting or being satisfied with the status quo.

Whether you think you can or think you can't, you're right. It's a choice you make, and it affects the team around you and even ripples beyond them. Choose wisely.

Rule 3. Don't confuse self-doubt with someone else's insecurity.

From a young age, we battle against others' insecurities. At the earliest of ages, our decisions aren't our own; they're made by someone else's belief in us. (This is typically a parent, guardian, or some other caregiver.) As we get older, however, we start making our own decisions, which are often grounded in our outlook of the world and belief in our abilities to operate in the world. Although our decisions may be our own at this point, we still rely on others' perceptions.

This reliance can either be a blessing or a curse. We care about what others think about us, and that can affect how we think about ourselves. Any negative or limiting perception others have of us can quickly imprison us in self-doubt and self-constraint.

Even in today's "everyone gets a trophy" world, we all battle limiting or deflating perceptions others have of us. Maybe it's because of the trophy society. Maybe there are other reasons. Regardless, it's important to know we can cast limiting assertions on others, just as they can upon us. Be aware that it happens, but don't let it manifest into your own self-doubt. Separate what's real from perception and what others think from what you believe. Your belief in yourself will overcome the self-doubt.

This is a rule and lesson shared by Suzie Smibert, the chief information security officer at Finning International. Specifically, she says to "have trust in yourself. Don't project your insecurity on others and don't let them project theirs onto you." Indeed!

Many of us were raised hearing, "You can do anything," and "You can be anybody." Some, however, grew up being questioned: "Who do you think you are to be dreaming like that?" "You'll never amount to anything!" "Who's going to want you?" In either reality, we'll need to overcome self-doubt and the insecurity we find others have in our abilities to realize our fullest potential.

Cheryl Smith said, "My goal in life was to be a CIO." Once she achieved that, her goal changed to wanting to be a CIO at a Fortune 50 company. She realized that goal as well. Cheryl's the former chief information officer of McKesson, which is among the top ten highest-revenue-generating companies in the United States—well within the Fortune 50.

To aim at being a CIO of a Fortune 50 company was a really big and bold goal for Cheryl—or for anyone, for that matter. There are only fifty positions you could be in to realize that goal, and to accomplish it means battling self-doubt and the insecurity others project upon you. Unfortunately, women will many times find additional battles and challenges on their journeys to realizing big goals, due to unconscious *and* conscious bias and blatant roadblocks from people who don't view them as capable in the executive suite.

We're fortunate to know Cheryl, and those she's worked with are fortunate that she achieved her goal, in part by never confusing self-doubt with someone else's insecurity about who she was, what she was doing, and the person she aspired to be. That's a lesson for all of us aiming to be continually better at what we do and who we are.

Just as you can't make someone else's decision, don't let someone else make yours—especially when it comes to your belief in yourself and the big, bold goals you aim to reach.

Rule 4. You may not get the chance to do a better job tomorrow.

A friend of ours is on the board of the Parkinson's Disease Foundation. We learned from him that Parkinson's is a particularly challenging disease because it affects *all* systems of the body. That's amazing, and devastating, to think about.

Like many battling Parkinson's, he has visible symptoms of the disease. When we met last summer, we enjoyed dinner together, reminisced about past experiences, and forecasted future ones. From our conversation, it became starkly clear that time is running out. The same is true, certainly in varying degrees, for all of us. So you've got to seize the day, because at some point, you won't have the chance to do a better job tomorrow.

Carpe diem—seize the day. Some of us became familiar with that phrase when the late Robin Williams said it in the movie *Dead Poets Society*. We hear this same sentiment in other phrases all the time. "Don't put off to tomorrow what you can do today" and "Don't procrastinate" are just a couple good reminders. Obviously, there are many others. The best leaders know the commodity of time, and they know there isn't an endless supply. Don't let time run out before you complete the things you want to achieve.

Think about your day. What's on your schedule? No doubt it's packed full. What are you putting off? What are you postponing, although you know you need to do it? Don't wait! All actions and reactions are important and are the reason this rule is part of the foundation of great leaders and leadership.

To illustrate this rule in a bit more detail, we'd like to share a story about Jan Dean, our good friend and the former executive director of a large and complex government agency. She gave us a unique perspective regarding time and its influence. She had just started a multiyear strategic initiative when she was diagnosed with cancer. It became clear to her that she may not be there at the end of the initiative. Believing in what she was doing and the people with whom she worked, she continued working at the agency and made sure everything she did was done with perfection and care. Status meetings, dashboard reporting, employee Q-and-A sessions, brown-bag lunches, and other interactions all took on a new meaning—a meaning like, "This presentation is going to be the best I've ever done," or "This e-mail correspondence is going to be the clearest one I've ever written," each implying "because it may be the last one."

After a few years and a lot of work, in parallel with a few rounds of chemotherapy, the initiative was very successful. In this instance, Jan was there to see the end. She retired from the agency, and shortly after that, she passed away. She was a truly exceptional leader.

You may not be there to see the end of whatever you're planning right now. Whether due to illness or any number of other reasons, you may not get the chance to do a better job tomorrow. The lesson from Jan is to work hard and expect to see the end but act as if you may not. Doing so will heighten your awareness of everything you do and the meaning behind it, especially with how you work with the people you encounter.

Mindset: Reflect, Review, and Commit

- What is your current mindset? Is a positive mindset part of your leadership foundation? Do you start something new with a belief that it can be done? Name a specific situation where your mindset needs to improve and at least two actions you can take toward improvement.
- Is there an area of your life or work where you doubt your own abilities? How is that constraining you? How might you go about things differently if you had more confidence and belief in yourself?
- In what ways do you experience self-doubt that's coming from the insecurity of others? How are you allowing others' perceptions of you to limit your potential? What needs to happen for you to increase belief in yourself and overcome the self-doubt stemming from others' insecurity?
- You just reflected on how your self-doubt is being influenced by others' insecurity. Consider ways you may be holding other people back because of *your* insecurity in *them.* What can you do to stop such behavior?
- What are two or three things on your to-do list that you just haven't gotten around to doing? How might it change your life, or someone else's, if you just got them done? If you knew your time was limited, what's the one thing you would ensure is completed? List at least one specific thing you can do today or this week that'll make your life, or someone else's, better. Make sure that thing gets done.

Purpose

Rule 5. Don't forget why you do what you do.

Think about how you spent the past day, week, or even month. Why did you spend it that way? Why did you invest your time the way you did? Did you go to work? Why do you go to work every day? Did you go to your daughter's recital or your son's play? Why? Did you get some exercise? Did you take your partner to lunch? Did you go to the neighborhood barbecue? Why?

On the surface, our answers to these questions may be simple: I go to work to make money so I can pay my bills and support a certain lifestyle for my family. I go to my kids' events to support them. I love my partner. I enjoy spending time with my neighbors. There may be deeper drivers for each of these decisions as well.

What did you do at work today? And why? Do you believe in what you're doing? Why? Do you care about the well-being, growth, and fulfillment of your coworkers, team, and colleagues? What about your customers and, beyond them, their families and communities?

If you don't know why you do what you do, then what you do will have limited purpose and limited fulfillment. Not knowing why you do what you do increases the possibility that you may be persuaded to do just about anything, for anyone, and for any reason.

Knowing your "why" is knowing your purpose. Knowing your why is knowing your cause. Knowing your why is knowing your point of view and perspective. Your why gives clarity in meaning to what you do. It's for this reason—at least in part—that the author and motivational speaker Simon Sinek wrote the books *Start with Why* and *Find Your Why* and the German philosopher Friedrich Nietzsche once said, "He who has a why can endure any how."

So what's your why? Why are you doing what you're doing?

As you think about your why, don't fall into the temptation of mediocrity or ease into the comfort of "good enough" due to any perceived constraints. In other words, don't settle for what seems like the obvious answer. You won't find your why there anyway. Rather, dive into the possibilities of abundance and full-potential performance to uncover the root of why you do what you do.

Again, think about how you spent your day. Why? Ask and answer the question *why* five times to get to the real reason. You may say:

"I spent my day working to make money." *Why?*
"Because I have bills to pay and a lifestyle to uphold for my family." *Why?*
"Because I want to be a good provider to them." *Why?*
"Because I want them to enjoy a good life." *Why?*
"Because I care for and love them." *Why?*
"Because when I see joy in them, I also have joy in who I am."

Now you know why you spend your days the way you do. And you probably already know the next logical question. Is that how you want to show up every day? If so, great! If that's the case for you, you've probably had an awesome day. If not, change it. Start now.

The best leaders live out their reason why every day. To know *what* you're doing is important, to know *how* you're going to do something is also important, but to know *why* you're doing something is most important. The best leaders understand that and share it with others on their teams and those they care for so they know why as well.

Rule 6. If you don't care, no one else will either.

Tim Callahan is a vice president at Aflac, a Fortune 500 insurance company. While he shuns bumper sticker philosophies, he believes the foundation of leadership is understanding that "people do not care what you know until they know how much you care." He understands that effective leadership requires an ability to care and a willingness to do so.

But an ability and willingness to care about *what?* The answer to this question is twofold: care about purpose and care about people. As a leader, you have to demonstrate that you care about what you're trying to achieve *and* about the people who are investing their time and effort to help you succeed.

Caring about what you're trying to achieve as a leader starts with demonstrating your passion for purpose and showing those who follow you that you care deeply about the realization of your ideas, mission, and goals. People may be intrigued with *what* you're trying to accomplish regardless of whether they actually believe in it themselves. Being intrigued by your ideas, however, won't guarantee that others will follow you and provide actionable support. In order to get that level of buy-in, those you wish to lead need to understand *why* you believe your ideas, mission, and goals are worth working for. In other words, they need to understand the purpose of what you're trying to accomplish. This requires you to be able to clearly communicate your why.

However, even a well-defined purpose is insufficient to fully enact buy-in and action. Through demonstration of passion, or deep caring for purpose, a leader can successfully convert *personal purpose* to *common purpose.* Passion motivates people and gives them a sense of belonging. Most importantly, passion for purpose gets a leader's team excited and motivated to take action. If team members are willing to commit their time and effort to take action without being commanded to do so, it indicates that they're truly committed to a common purpose.

Without commitment from his or her team, a leader's ideas, mission, and goals won't be realized. Success is a team sport, and because of this, showing you care about the people on your team is the second important aspect of caring leadership. Author and leadership guru Dale Carnegie said, "You can make more friends in two months by becoming interested in other people than you can in two years by trying to get other people interested in you." The point Carnegie makes here is that showing you care for the people on your team inspires loyalty. That loyalty, in turn, leads to increased productivity, increased team morale, and decreased turnover—all important variables needed to achieve goals and accomplish a common purpose.

When leaders demonstrate a sincere caring for the people they lead, they're creating a culture of support for their teams, organizations, and enterprises. In creating a culture of support, caring for people becomes about ensuring individual perspectives and contributions are supported and team members are empowered to positively influence their work and work environment. Team members see that their leader not only supports their ideas but also takes action to do something with those ideas. As a result, team members will take ownership of their actions relative to the expected outcomes. This is what it really means to have alignment and commitment to a common purpose.

If you know an effective leader, the odds are good that you've found someone with the ability and willingness to demonstrate that he or she cares and why. You've also found someone who understands the true power of caring when it comes to both purpose and people.

Rule 7. Know what you're willing to give.

Important things get done only when capital is spent. Therefore, if you're going to get anything important done, you're going to invest capital. Think about it. If you're going to realize a financial return, you've got to invest sweat equity (personal capital of time and muscle) or financial equity (money capital). If you're going to build a lasting friendship, you've got to invest emotional capital and time. If you're going to build a strong partnership, you've got to invest in mutual-gains capital. Whatever it is that you aim to accomplish, you've got to invest. You've got to give something, and that something will be of value.

Think about that the next time you say, "I don't have enough time to have my one-on-one with John today because I have to get this status report turned in," or "I don't have the resources necessary to invest in that person or that other person or even myself." In all situations, you're making decisions about what you're going to give and why.

It's not by accident that this rule—*know what you're willing to give*—comes after *don't forget why you do what you do* and *if you don't care, no one else will either.* It's about knowing purpose, prioritizing the most important over someone else's urgent, and knowing your investment and expected return. Your time spent throughout the day should be viewed the same way. If you want to realize a positive gain in something, you're going to have to invest. Your biggest chore or challenge may be determining what to invest in, or it may be what *not* to invest time and energy in. It's for this reason that H. L. Hunt, the Texas oil tycoon and political activist, said, "Decide what you want, decide what you are willing to exchange for it. Establish your priorities and go to work." That's good advice.

Know what's important, and invest in only those things. This sentiment and this rule remind us of the old Cherokee story "Two Wolves," which illustrates the battle we engage in every day. The story is told by an old Cherokee who was teaching his grandson about life. "A fight is going on inside me," he said to the boy. "It is a terrible fight, and it is between two wolves. One is evil—he is anger, envy, sorrow, regret, greed, arrogance, self-pity, guilt, resentment, inferiority, lies, false pride, superiority, and ego." He continued, "The other is good—he is joy, peace, love, hope, serenity, humility, kindness, benevolence, empathy, generosity, truth, compassion, and faith. The same fight is going on inside you—and inside every other person, too."

The grandson thought about it for a minute and then asked his grandfather, "Which wolf will win?"

The old Cherokee replied simply, "The one you feed."

Like everyone, your capital is limited. So know what you want to do, why, what you're willing to give, what you're going to invest in, and what you're *not* going to invest in. Know what you're going to feed. When you know what's most important to feed, your capital is invested in your purpose—and rightfully so.

Rule 8. The purpose of business is people serving people.

Tom Peters is known for a lot of things. He's a former partner of McKinsey & Company's organizational effectiveness practice. He's written a number of books, of which our favorite is *In Search of Excellence.* He's a dynamic speaker who leverages keen observations, research, and experiences to help make leaders better. He's a genuine leadership guru, and he gets it right more often than not. We're big fans, especially when it comes to his perspective on the purpose of business. It's "people serving people, period."

Rosabeth Moss Kanter is the author of *Supercorp: How Vanguard Companies Create Innovation, Profits, Growth, and Social Good.* Her research supports Peters's claim and our belief. She found that a company's core purpose is more than just making money; it's about accomplishing a societal purpose. The best organizations, and the leaders within them, know that to be successful at serving people at a societal level requires being great at serving one another at the organizational level.

At the core of any business is a theoretical hypothesis of people helping people. Whether with a product or a service, businesses are organized with people serving other people.

Not everyone immediately appreciates this concept. Some believe organizations are formed simply to maximize shareholder wealth. This philosophy wasn't developed from the creative mind of a Hollywood writer on assignment to craft one-liners for the greed-obsessed Gordon Gekko character in the movie *Wall Street.* It was actually a court ruling. In 1919, the Michigan State Supreme Court argued that the primary purpose of an organization was profit for shareholders. This decision informed the actions of many executives when it came to either paying or withholding shareholders' stock dividends. It's also from this case that "shareholder maximization" and "maximization of shareholder wealth" became widely known phrases and accepted as the purpose of business. However, the core of maximization of shareholder value is people (resources within a business) serving other people (stockholders, stakeholders, coworkers, and customers) to maximize their benefit. Tom Peters and Rosabeth Moss Kanter got it right again.

Great leaders know that the purpose of business has an even greater responsibility than just investor gain. It's a responsibility beyond the business itself. It's a responsibility relative to being part of a greater system. Sure, there are employees, customers, and shareholders, but then there are their families, friends, and communities that stretch far beyond the core of any business.

As you think about your business, think beyond the office walls. Think beyond shareholders. Think to those consuming your goods and services. Think to the connections your employees have in the community, their families, and their even farther-reaching connections. The purpose of any business is relative to all of them, a larger system, and is grounded in the act of people serving people—period.

Rule 9. The purpose of people is finding meaning in work.

It's one thing to know the purpose of business—people serving people—but to be fully effective as a leader, you have to know the purpose of people. Every individual wants to be part of an awesome team and the products and reputations that go along with that. To realize this, you have to focus the impact you have on people.

The most effective leaders give people a sense of purpose. They empower people to do their best work, and they have a bias of action toward making positive experiences happen for the people around them with each and every interaction—from an e-mail to a phone call to a hallway conversation. Their aim is to instill a sense of meaning in people by being engaged with something truly exceptional.

So what's the best advice we've learned? Amy Messersmith, the chief people officer at TDIndustries, said, "My best advice is to err on the side of treating people like people." Agreed! To do so, you've got to know people. The best way to do that, according to David Bray, the chief information officer at the Federal Communications Commission, is to "seek to understand what brings people joy." Gary Warzala, a senior vice president at PNC Financial Services Group, says, "Your relationships are personal and because of that you've got to make sure people know that you sincerely care." To do this, Dave Estlick, a senior vice president at Starbucks, says to "lead through the lens of humanity; respect the individual and protect the individual." This is the core of what leadership is and what great leaders do: they make work personal because they create purpose for people in their work.

Ryan Russell is the director of human-centered design at Amazon. He has a unique and effective way to set this tone among his team. During new-employee orientation, he meets with each member of his team individually. Doing so is certainly not a unique practice, but what he says and asks during these meetings are. He says, "I'd like to address the elephant in the room. You and I both know that this is not going to be your last job or the last company that you're going to work for, but I am committed to making it the best. It's up to us to make it the best. What can I do to make it the best?" We each can have similar conversations with our employees, and as it does for Ryan and his team, it can set the tone for employees to find meaning in their work and know they have their leader's support to make their time there awesome, while also preparing them for their next move.

Additionally, the best leaders ask, listen to, and thank the people around them. They, like Ryan and the others we've mentioned, create opportunities and experiences in which people can succeed. Cathie Brow, the senior vice president of human resources at Revera, explains it this way: "People are people, and the same things motivate them everywhere. It's understanding their role, feeling like they make a difference, feeling appreciated by their boss, and reporting to a great leader who inspires them." The purpose of people is to find meaning in their work, dedicate their time to doing great work, and see their work as valuable to others. Your role as a leader is to enable that experience.

Rule 10. Leadership is art, and you sign your name to it every day.

Perhaps the best definition of leadership we've ever heard came from Colin Powell. He defined it this way: "Leadership is the art of getting more accomplished from a team of people than the science of management says is possible." That's eloquent, insightful, and accurate.

First of all, leadership is art. You may have heard that before. Think about how many decisions leaders make every day. Answers to most of those decisions can't be found in some textbook or field guide. Think about all the decisions made where swinging too far one way or the other is problematic. Consider all the situations where a cookie-cutter approach doesn't work because people are unique and must be addressed uniquely. Unlike many aspects of management, there's no scientific formula for leadership. Leadership is art and therefore involves artistic maneuvers and creative thinking.

Colton Janes, the director of operations at Aqua America, explained the importance of thinking of leadership as art to us. He said, "Knowing that leadership is an art makes you—the leader—an artist. Just like all artists, you sign your name to your work in every meeting, in every product design, in everything you do every day. Your name is attached to what you do." Veresh Sita, the chief information officer at Alaska Airlines, expressed a similar sentiment: "Take so much pride in what you do that you're willing to carve your initials into it every day."

Have you ever thought of your leadership in that way? It's a rather powerful way to consider your role as a leader. You're an artist. Your management work is based in science. It's about head stuff, intellectual quotient (or IQ) stuff. Your leadership work, on the other hand, is art. It's about heart stuff, emotional quotient (or EQ) stuff. Daniel Goleman wasn't the first to study the power of EQ, but he did popularize it with his best-selling book *Emotional Intelligence: Why It Can Matter More Than IQ*.

While IQ focuses largely on academic abilities and measures cognitive capacity, EQ is a reflection of one's ability to empathize with others; express and control emotions, especially in difficult or stressful situations; and understand others' emotional meaning. It's EQ, not IQ, that enables us to connect with others and lead effectively.

It's important to know that regardless of whether you sign your name to your work every day, people do it on your behalf based on their connection with you. You influence everyone who sees and hears you every day. They attach your name to what they perceive. So whether you want to sign your name to your work every day (and throughout every day) or not, it's there. It's the art you've created based on the impact you've had on others, and your initials are carved into it for everyone to see. Keep this in mind as you go about your day. Keep in mind that every action you take is accompanied by your signature; it's a reflection of your leadership and ultimately a reflection of who you are as a colleague and a person.

As you power down your computer after each day's work or as you make your commute home, think about your work of art for that day. Did you get more from your team than the science of management says is possible? Did you inspire the team members to accomplish more than they thought was possible? Did you create a lasting, positive impact on each of your team members? Did you help them understand their roles and let them know they make a difference and are appreciated? Are you proud to sign your work of art?

You sign your name to the work you do as a leader every day. Be a proud artist. Be a great leader!

Purpose: Reflect, Review, and Commit

- Think about why you do what you do. What's the meaning in your work? In short, what's the purpose in what you do? What's the significance in it for you? Perform the five-why exercise described in rule 5 by first asking, "Why do I spend my day the way I do?" Ask and answer the question "Why?" five times to uncover the root of why. Once that's complete, consider how you might take this personal meaning from your work and help others to see the purpose in their work. How can you better enable people to find meaning in the work they do?
- List three things you did during the past week. Briefly describe the "why" behind each of these activities. Does the prioritization of these activities change after considering the why? Using this logic, reprioritize the things currently on your to-do list to assure the most important items are ranked appropriately.
- Think about the business you're in and the company you work for. How would you describe the purpose of your work? Does it involve people serving people? If not, can you think of ways to include service to people within that purpose? In your specific role, what people do you serve, and what are some steps you can take to serve with even greater impact?
- How might seeing your leadership as a work of art change the way you go about it? Are there a few things that happened this past week that you're really glad your name is signed to? What caused those things to happen? Equally, what happened this week that you wish your name weren't signed to? What caused those things to happen? What might you do differently going forward, now that you know you're an artist and sign your name to your work every day?

Perspective

Rule 11. Your perspective may be yours alone.

The grass is green. The sky is blue. Planes fly in the sky. Right? How about pizza being the best food on Earth and 1980s hair bands creating the best music ever? It's not as easy to agree on these last two arguments. Why? It's about perspective. We see and experience the world in different ways. In more academic terms, our mental models are uniquely created from life experiences and explain to us how the world works and why. Our experiences uniquely qualify us to view the world through a specific lens: our own. Unfortunately, the stakes are often higher than just agreeing on the best food to eat and music to listen to with friends, family, and colleagues.

Have you ever left a meeting completely assured that everyone else leaving that same meeting knew exactly what to do only to return to chaos a few days later? Have you ever had a conversation with a frustrated employee who you thought was generously empowered only to find he or she was struggling with a sense of having no empowerment at all? What about a situation where some members of the team agree the work is done while you still see the project as incomplete? These realities highlight just how often we can find ourselves in situations where our perspectives may not be universally shared.

Many people go through life thinking the way they see the world is universal—that everyone else sees the world the same as they do. Hardly. Mark Twain once said, "It's not what you don't know that kills you. It's what you know for sure that ain't true." Perceptions become individual truths that are used to guide decisions, behavior, and actions. When perspectives differ, challenges arise, and success can be compromised.

One of the best lessons in life is the one that creates awareness of one's own bias. Different people see the world differently in different situations. It's like how you didn't like brussels sprouts as a kid but do now. Similarly, it's how one person can see a Picasso painting and be filled with emotion while another person is left feeling indifferent about it. Or how one person may argue that Porsche makes the finest sports cars in the world while another thinks they're just slightly modified Volkswagens.

Perspectives matter. We all have perspective—it's the lens through which we see and interpret the world. And, yes, as we've all likely heard before, perception is reality. But it's important to know, too, that your perspective—your reality—may be yours alone.

As with the examples just provided, your perspective may be your reality. No doubt it is. But it certainly doesn't equate to universal truth. It's for this reason that communication and alignment among teams are so important. Making sure you see problems, challenges, products, solutions, and visions the same is important. So keep in mind that your perception may be yours alone and that you'll need to diagnose differences and build alignment with others if you want to succeed.

The best leaders work not to simply impose their perceptions on others but to understand others' perceptions and work to build agreement on how things currently are and what they aim to do together. Roland Cloutier, the chief security officer at ADP and the author of *Becoming a Global Chief Security Executive Officer: A How-To*

Guide for Next Generation Security Leaders, reminded us of this: "Alignment drives connection and the way you get things done is through human connection." The only way to establish human connection is to understand and align individual perspectives.

Rule 12. Have a point of view, but be willing to change it.

It could be argued that the worst thing anyone can have is an opinion without a point of view. Always, always, always have a point of view. Know why you claim a certain perspective or opinion. Be able to articulate it along with alternatives. That's having a point of view. And recognize that your point of view is *your* point of view and may not be shared by everyone—and that's okay. In fact, your point of view may not even be true. Remember, "It's not what you don't know that kills you. It's what you know for sure that ain't true." It's for this reason that Dave Estlick from Starbucks said, "My best advice is to have a point of view, but don't die on your point of view."

To be effective, you must know the connection between your opinion and perspective. To do this, you must understand both contextual and situational conditions of your argument. And you also must be willing, and therefore humble enough, to not die on your point of view, because your point of view may not be right relative to alternatives from others.

Too many people focus on being right. Be humble in the fact you may be wrong. The key is not in being right but in getting it right—there's a big difference. Points of view create conversations and allow for multiple alternatives to be created. So while your point of view may very well get challenged and ultimately may be determined not to be right because of alternatives that are better, sharing your point of view effectively most likely helps in getting it right—the solution, the answer, the way forward.

Colleen Wood, the chief human resources officer at LivingSocial, explains it simply: "Take ownership. Be authentic.

Bring a point of view." Different points of view bring different voices to the table, and the more diverse you all are, the smarter you'll be collectively. Bringing multiple points of view increases the likelihood of getting it right.

Make sure you contribute effectively by having a point of view. You should have a point of view and a clear perspective of what creates your opinions and drives your behaviors. But remember rule 11: *your perspective may be yours alone.* While it's important to have a point of view, it's equally important to have the humility to not die on your point of view.

Rule 13. Stop believing everything you think.

Marshall Goldsmith, a prolific author and highly respected and successful executive coach, has done some research on mindset, purpose, and perspective. Some of his research has uncovered this interesting finding: 70 percent of people believe they're in the top 10 percent of performers, 82 percent of people believe they're in the top 20 percent, and 98.5 percent of people believe they're in the top half. That's crazy, right? You don't need to know much about math to know these numbers simply don't work. What's on display here is simple overconfidence and an inflated view of self-worth.

You may be familiar with the concept of overconfidence bias, which often is labeled the overconfidence effect. Psychologists Howard Raiffa and Marc Alpert have done much work studying this concept—what it is, how it's created, and the effects of having such a bias. Possibly the easiest way to define the overconfidence effect is by considering the difference between what people think they know and what they really know. That's the overconfidence effect in action. We also may call it what it is more simply: delusion.

Think about your leadership. Are you a great boss, a great leader? Are you someone who meets regularly with your staff?

Someone who listens intently? Do you do a good job of providing support and empowerment? Are you consistently present and available? Do you exemplify positive nonverbal behaviors when you're in meetings? Are you a polished speaker who presents in concise and easy-to-understand ways? We hope you said yes to all of these questions; however, there's a reality hidden here: just because you think you are an accomplished leader, it doesn't mean it's true. It could be a delusion. You could suffer from overconfidence bias and, on occasion, probably do.

We're always going to think. That's the way we're made. Our brains are constantly processing and making sense of the world. But how we make sense of the world and ourselves may not be true. This leadership rule (life rule, really!) points to the fact that sometimes we can get in our own way by creating stories that simply aren't real.

It's tough to gauge the accuracy of our thoughts without measuring them against facts and perspectives from others, especially those who have different ways of thinking and making sense of the world. As you go about your important work, constantly check your perspective against others' and help others to do the same. Doing so can help us understand if what we think is what we should believe or if we simply have it wrong because of an overconfidence effect or delusion.

Constantly check what you think. Know there will be times when you'll need to stop believing what you think because it's simply not true.

Rule 14. No one has all the answers all the time.

Once, after coming out of a boardroom, we heard an executive say, "If I'm the smartest person in that room, we're in trouble." To be honest, the executive most likely *was* the smartest person in that room, but that wasn't the lesson to be learned from her comment. The lesson from her comment is one of humility. She realized there likely were things she didn't know. Because of that, she embraced the spirit of collaboration and dependence on those she leads to fill in her knowledge gaps. She knew she didn't have all the answers all the time. No one ever does. No one's right all the time—that includes her, us, and you, too! She leveraged this knowledge by making sure she had the right questions to get to the right answers. She was focused more on getting it right than being right.

Barry Melnkovic, the executive vice president and chief human resources officer at US Steel, asked a very good question on this same subject: "Would you rather be known as the person with all the right answers or the leader with all the right questions?" Hopefully you said the latter.

You've got to know that your present knowledge is imperfect at best. It's what drives a mindset of collaboration and continual learning: two critical aspects of great leadership. It also speaks to the importance of humility on the part of a leader, which when present, enables him or her to be open to other perspectives, ways of seeing the world, and ways of doing things. Yanni Charalambous, a vice president at Occidental Petroleum, may have expressed the importance of humility best: "I'll never know everything. Recognizing that opens up an opportunity to seek leadership in people around you who can provide insights where you have gaps."

We all have gaps—knowledge gaps, awareness gaps, perspective gaps—and each one prevents us from ever having all the answers. Appreciate this reality and surround yourself with good people who can help you get the answers you need to make better decisions and be a better leader.

Perspective: Reflect, Review, and Commit

- Document a recent time when you realized others didn't share your perspective. What kind of problem(s) did this create? Write down a few ideas of how you can sort out your own perspectives from those of others and how you can work to better understand people.

- When recognizing the need to collaborate and surround yourself with good people to succeed, with whom do you need to deepen your relationship? Who do you need to thank for investing in and supporting you? Who might you be able to support at a greater level to encourage their success? Do it!

- Consider an upcoming meeting that you'll either lead or be a part of. Given the agenda for that meeting, outline your points of view relative to the items that'll be addressed. Also, attempt to document other possible points of view attendees at that meeting might hold. By understanding multiple points of view, how will you be more effective in the meeting?

- Write down some areas where you might believe something that isn't really true. Be very honest with yourself. How might you be able to confirm or dismiss this notion? Who can you talk with in the next week to get honest feedback relative to these possible inaccuracies?

- Given the fact that you won't be right all the time, how do you go about making sure you get it right? Document a few opportunities related to your answer to the previous question. How might your perspective need to change for you to better work with the people around you?

Section 1: Station Break

As you can tell by this point, *My Best Advice* isn't an academic text to labor through; it's a workbook. Now's a great time in your hypothetical journey from Seattle to Chicago to pull back. Pause, reflect, and talk with your friends, neighbors, colleagues, and other leaders about where you are and where you're going.

At this point, you're fourteen rules into this journey and have thoroughly covered the foundation of great leaders and leadership. If you're envisioning your journey on Amtrak, you've traveled beyond the eastern border of Washington State and are already through Sandpoint, the only station stop in Idaho. You may be at the station stop in Essex, Montana. Or maybe you've made it to West Glacier near Glacier National Park, which you would find sits at more than three thousand feet in elevation. The only thing that keeps the mountain peaks you can see from the western entrance of the park from crumbling is their foundation. The same is true for leaders—a leader's foundation determines the peak of his or her performance. So this station stop in your journey is a perfect place to think about and study the foundation of your leadership: your mindset, your purpose, and your perspective.

Because your mindset, purpose, and perspective are the grounding of leadership, we call this the foundation. Spend some time here to truly understand your foundation; only from understanding it will you be able to understand what you believe is possible and what you can achieve because of that belief.

While you think about the last fourteen rules, consider the following:

- Which rules really resonated with you? How do you intend to put these into practice this week or within the next thirty days?
- Which rules of your own might you add to this section on foundation? How are they relevant to where you are currently and what you see as possible in the future?

Your success as a leader will be made possible only by the strength and efficacy of your leadership foundation. That's been the focus of this station break.

Section 2
The Pillars of Great Leaders and Leadership

Most great leaders we think of are people we'd describe as successful. They achieve amazing results and accomplish big goals; however, as they go about their work, there's no guarantee of their success. Regardless of how positive their mindset, purpose, and perspective are, there are simply too many competing factors to guarantee success for these leaders. The same is true for each of us. We have no claim, guarantee, or entitlement to realizing amazing results, achieving big goals, or being the least bit successful. Yet the great leaders we think of do so regularly. Part of the reason for their success is that they understand that their only guarantee is in the work they do and how they do it every day.

Our work leads to our outcomes, and outcomes determine success. Enabling factors, such as a foundation of positive leadership, can help, but you need more than that to be successful. The best leaders we know have three pillars of focus that rise up from their strong leadership foundations to strengthen everything they do and everything their teams work to accomplish. These pillars of leadership include *vision, preparation,* and *action.* We've divided seventeen rules among these three pillars; when effectively applied, they'll increase your probability of achieving big goals, amazing results, and overall success.

Vision
Rule 15.   Greatness is never achieved while maintaining the status quo.

Rule 16.   Don't fall victim to fear disguised as practicality.

Rule 17.   Setting and realizing a vision is hard, not impossible.

Preparation
Rule 18.   Hope is not a strategy.

Rule 19.   Don't mistake a clear vision with a short distance.

Rule 20.   If you're going to succeed, you've got to prioritize.

Rule 21. Small details never are.

Rule 22. Excellence is not an exception.

Action

Rule 23. Err on the side of action.

Rule 24. You don't need unanimous consent to move forward.

Rule 25. Don't confuse effort with progress or output with outcomes.

Rule 26. Don't get your actions ahead of your culture's readiness to act.

Rule 27. However bad you think it is, it's not as bad as you think.

Rule 28. Play both defense and offense.

Rule 29. Measure what matters—only what matters.

Rule 30. Don't let yesterday's frustrations hijack today's successes.

Rule 31. Did I do my absolute best today?

Becoming the leader you aim to be and achieving the goals you aspire to reach first requires a clear vision of the future. This vision provides clarity regarding what the future looks like. It's a described future state you can realize by achieving strategic goals, endeavors, and dreams. When expressed properly, the vision is aspirational, inspirational, and motivational. It can also be quite scary. Ellen Johnson Sirleaf, the author of *This Child Will Be Great: Memoir of a Remarkable Life by Africa's First Woman President*, said, "If your dreams do not scare you, they are not big enough." The best leaders know that your dreams, those goals you aspire to accomplish, need to be big in order to inspire and motivate. Otherwise great leaders might refrain from such audacity due to perceived risk and fear. You'll learn from the rules about vision that limiting your goals keeps you not only from reaching success but also from being truly satisfied. Remember, part of rule 1 is *it can be done.* Vision is connected to mindset, and it's for this reason that the first rule in this section is *greatness is never achieved while maintaining the status quo.* To achieve greatness and personal satisfaction, you'll need to assume some risk and overcome perhaps quite a bit of fear as you chase down your goals, endeavors, and dreams. But know that while, yes, it's hard, it's not impossible. The great leaders we think of do it regularly. So can you!

To mitigate risk and fear associated with scary goals, the best leaders emphasize preparation. Whether your big goal is learning to play the guitar well enough to perform in front of a live audience or leading a team through a major organizational change to gain greater effectiveness and scale, you'll need proper preparation to realize your envisioned future state. Part of the logic pointing to the need for such preparation is understood by the fact that neither of these two goals—or any others you aim to accomplish, for that matter—will be realized in one giant leap or one fell swoop. It's going to take a lot of work. It's going to take time. To organize your work over any period of time, you need to plan, to prioritize, and to set appropriate expectations. That's all part of leadership preparation.

It's from preparation that you, the leader, galvanize your commitment to the vision and align your team's commitment to that vision as well as to one another's success in reaching it. That means action. Being and staying paralyzed in preparation does nothing toward realizing big goals. Proper preparation, however, fuels excitement to engage in efforts aligned with those goals. That's the action you want and need to succeed!

While action is what you want, it's when in action that individual and team commitment will begin to be challenged and the leader's foundation will be tested. The truth is, the best plans are theoretical models of an anticipated set of moving variables, and because they're moving, your plan won't be enough to reach any goal if it's transfixed to the point of being immobile. You'll need to adapt along the way if you're going to succeed. This can be as scary, or more so, as the big goal itself. The best leaders don't let that stop them from moving forward. They err on the side of action to prevent from getting stuck. They measure progress relative to the goal, make adjustments as needed, and rely on the strength of their positive leadership foundation to prevent any frustration from hijacking their success. They're perpetually optimistic and focus on how best to show up every day and face the world as they find it.

Building upon the foundation of section 1, section 2 details the practices of great leaders and leadership. Before reading these seventeen rules, pause here for a moment to think about your leadership. Think about your dreams and goals. Are they big enough? Are they scary? This section will help to determine if they are and help you clarify a *vision*, understand the need for proper *preparation*, and decide how best to enable *action*, which together serve as the three pillars of focus in your leadership foundation.

As you did throughout section 1, consider each rule carefully, mark those you want to adopt as your own, share your new lessons and key takeaways with others, and document your own rules that, when put into practice, will make you an even better leader.

Vision

Rule 15. Greatness is never achieved while maintaining the status quo.

The best leaders have a general philosophy that things can always be better. Spend any amount of time with Yanni Charalambous, a vice president at Occidental Petroleum, and you'll hear him say, "Good enough isn't good enough if it can be better, and better isn't good enough if it can be great." This is true because good enough is often translated into just enough, adequate, fine, or status quo. Status quo is never good enough, because achieving status quo doesn't enable you to get better. Nor does it equate to achieving big goals.

One of life's simple maxims is this: "If you always do what you've always done, you'll always get what you've always gotten." Henry Ford used to say that, and Mark Twain and Tony Robbins had their own versions as did Steven Harvey, a senior vice president at HSBC North American Holdings, who said, "Challenge the status quo. Are we doing something because we've always done it or can we do something better? Can we do it faster, can we do it more efficiently, can we do it cheaper?" The message here is to set a vision beyond good enough, beyond the status quo, which is exactly the advice from Wes Hargrove, the senior vice president of development at 7-Eleven, who said, "As a leader, you've got to challenge the status quo." It's useful to keep this in mind as you consider your goals and cast your vision of a future state.

As a leader, you want to think beyond the status quo to something big, because great things never come from maintaining the status quo. Now, to be sure, there are times when keeping the status quo may seem like a big goal and a big win. Taking the long view, however, maintaining the status quo is a losing proposition. Take this advice from Gary Wimberly, a senior vice president at Express Scripts: "What's gotten us where we are won't allow us to be successful in the future." That's great advice to keep in mind. Executive coach Marshall Goldsmith wrote an entire book on this topic, *What Got You Here Won't Get You There*. To get "there" (any future state) from "here" requires change in our current state, not maintaining the status quo of it. It requires a vision that's big and bold—and, as you'll recall from section 1, a mindset that knows achieving it is possible. Whether we're aiming for personal greatness, which will require personal growth and behavioral change, or organizational greatness, which will require market growth and new innovation, the condition isn't status quo; it's *big* change.

It's equally important to note here that your personal satisfaction as a leader is dependent upon change. Your satisfaction will never be realized by maintaining the status quo. To really understand this, let's think about Michelangelo di Lodovico Buonarroti Simoni (now you understand why he's known simply as *Michelangelo*) for a moment. He's famous for a great number of things. Certainly, his ability as a sculptor, painter, architect, and poet likely come to mind. He's also known for his teachings to set big goals. He said, "The greater danger for most of us lies not in setting our aim too high and falling short; but in setting our aim too low, and achieving our mark." Ask yourself, are your goals set too low? Is your vision set to maintain the status quo or on achieving a big goal? Are the goals big enough that they scare you?

Instead of status quo, think *big!* Your barometer to know if your goal's big enough is whether it scares you. If the vision, goals, and dreams you have don't scare you, then they're not nearly big enough. It takes big goals to achieve and realize greatness and personal satisfaction.

Rule 16. Don't fall victim to fear disguised as practicality.

In a 2014 commencement speech, actor and funnyman Jim Carrey said, "Many of us choose our path out of fear disguised as practicality." It's easy to rationalize such behavior. As we journey, we'll be confronted with situations where we'll risk failure and loss. As we do, we'll find ourselves having to confront our fears. It could be fear of the unknown, fear of failure, or any number of other points of anxiety. Fear is the human emotion that naturally occurs and tries to move us to higher likelihood of safety by creating a mindset of self-doubt. It's easy to see how the practicality of setting a vision of status quo is more reasonable than anything bigger—especially anything a lot bigger—because it's less scary. Fear can prevent us from casting a big vision, and it can seduce any leader into believing practicality is a big bet. But it's not.

Fear, indeed, can be paralyzing if it permeates and shapes our mindset. At the same time, however, we can harness that emotion and energy to have it invigorate our vision casting. In this regard, fear isn't all bad. In fact, it can actually be really good for us as leaders and for our teams. The fear we face can provide the motivation needed to overcome a challenge and to reach a new plateau, if harnessed properly.

Mark Zuckerberg, the chairman and chief executive officer at Facebook, said, "The biggest risk is not taking any risk...In a world that is changing really quickly, the only strategy that is guaranteed to fail is not taking risks." So what are you prepared to do?

No doubt, if you intend to cast a big vision and chase down big goals—the ones that are truly scary—you'll certainly confront risk and face fear. It's unavoidable. Risk is unavoidable, and therefore facing fear is also unavoidable. Most everything we want to achieve in life and career requires us to face fear and move beyond it to the outer fringes of our comfort zone. To succeed at the highest levels and accomplish the biggest goals, the best leaders use fear as a measure of continual improvement.

To be a great leader, you must embrace change and view risk as an opportunity to do something greater than what's easy and often perceived as most practical. You must be willing to pivot, improve, and ready yourself and your team for the next decision, challenge, lesson to be learned, and accomplishment to be celebrated. Don't get stuck in analysis paralysis or thinking that a prior decision is a single and final act. Indeed, risk is unavoidable because change is unavoidable, but don't let that stop you from being effective.

Our fear can fool us into believing greatness is found along the journey of practicality, but it's not. When fear is the only obstacle you face, be courageous. Choose courage over comfort, because success begins right outside your comfort zone, and you get there only by not falling victim to fear.

Rule 17. Setting and realizing a vision is hard, not impossible.

We've mentioned that if you always do what you've always done, you'll always get what you've always gotten. This is a losing proposition because everyone and every organization is looking to get better. When it comes to needing to get better, whether that need is due to advancements in technology, global market pressures, fluctuating economies, customer demands, shifts in employee demographics, or other variables, your need to change is inevitable. And if you've ever tried to bring about change in anything, you know it's hard. The Harvard Business School professor and guru of organizational-change management John Kotter said, "Guiding change may be the ultimate test of a leader." That's true.

Over the years, we've asked dozens of seasoned executives and effective change agents why change is so hard. A great explanation came from Marc Varner, the global chief information security officer at YUM! Brands. He said, "Change is hard because, like water and electricity, people follow the path of least resistance." People like comfort. They like predictability. They like to know what's going on and what's going to happen. This, in part, is what separates great leaders from everyone else. The best leaders are those who know that greatness isn't found along the path of least resistance but in their ability to cast a compelling vision of a future state and help others navigate there together. This is the opposite of least resistance. It's the most difficult. It's the ultimate test of a leader.

While change is hard, it's important to know that change is not impossible. Here's how you can increase your likelihood of success with the change endeavors necessary to realize your envisioned future state:

- Spend time among those you're asking to change to help write the compelling vision and reason for the change.
- Gain the support of upper, lower, and lateral managers—you're going to need it.
- Keep the big vision always in mind but proceed with small, incremental steps toward your goal.
- Aim for early wins and continual wins along the journey.
- Broadcast those wins in celebratory fashion to build momentum over time.

John Kotter and others have found that when these efforts are implemented effectively, they dramatically increase the probability of you and your team successfully overcoming the challenges of change and realizing envisioned future-state goals.

Before leaving this rule, let us offer a bit more about the importance of communication. The communication aspects of bringing about change and realizing a big vision will seem overwhelming. As the leader, you'll often wonder why you need to keep explaining the vision and need for the change. The answer to that question is that people affected by the change won't embrace the rationale and adopt the change at the same time or for the same reason. You'll have early adopters, and you'll have laggards, and you'll likely have some who will never adopt the change at all. John Marcante, the chief information officer at Vanguard, said, "You always have to communicate and reiterate—many more times than you would think is necessary." When you think you have communicated to the point where you can't possibly have to say it again, communicate it at least two more times, and then you're likely *almost* to the point where people understand and can communicate it themselves to others.

Realizing your vision is grounded in effective communication. It needs to be aspiring, inspiring, and motivating. In short, your communication needs to be compelling, consistent, and always focused on bringing about increased clarity, confidence, and community. And you'll need to communicate the vision of the future, how you're going to get there, and the importance of each person in realizing that future state often. Without effective communication and the efforts noted above, your chances to realize your vision will be derailed by resistance. This blueprint illustrates and highlights the difficulty of leading change and the possibility of successfully doing so.

Vision: Reflect, Review, and Commit

- Are your current goals set to maintain the status quo or to achieve something much greater? What goals do you have right now that scare you? If you don't have any stretch goals, take the time to identify at least one to achieve within the next six months.
- What's an area in your personal or professional life where you need to experience transformation, to make a big bet? What's the end goal, and how will you measure success along the way? Who do you need to communicate with to give yourself every opportunity for success? Plan for that success now and identify early wins that can build momentum toward realizing your goal.
- What fear is holding you back? What decision(s) do you need to make where you don't have all the facts, which may be keeping you from action? What's a courageous action you need to take right now to move forward? Plan to take that action within the next month.

Preparation

Rule 18. Hope is not a strategy.

Most successful people readily acknowledge the role that luck plays in their success. Let's face it: sometimes we just catch a break and get lucky. It happens, and we can celebrate when it does; however, to use a phrase made popular by former New York City mayor Rudy Giuliani, "Hope is not a strategy."

Chance, good fortune, serendipity, coincidence, and maybe even luck all come into play in work and life. However, to have hope and nothing more is not a path to success. No doubt miracles happen every day, but to rely solely on them is foolish. It's good to have an active plan for success that can be made even better when elements of luck and chance do fall in our favor.

Having said that, it's important to recognize the role that hope *does* play regarding strategy without confusing it as strategy itself. Hope is a critical part of achieving a strategy because, at its core, hope is connected to having a positive mindset in that it's the belief that something is possible and probable to occur. As humans, we can't survive without hope. A mindset of abundance over scarcity never takes place without having a seed of hope. So hope definitely is requisite when it comes to our preparation of work toward our personal and team vision.

Hope alone, however, is wishful thinking. No one can wish his or her way to effectiveness, greatness, success, or any desired future state. As the Greek poet Achilochus said, "We don't rise to the level of our expectations. We fall to the level of our training." Our outcomes are realized only through concentrated effort of training, planning and preparation, and then follow-through. Knowing this, we can also know that one's luck is often a veil hiding significant preparation.

Those noting luck as part of their success realize it's just that: a *part* of something more. When digging a bit deeper into their success, you quickly find that there's much more preparation correlated with success as compared to just plain luck. After ten years of research, Richard Wiseman, the author of *The Luck Factor: The Scientific Study of the Lucky Mind*, found "to a large extent, people make their own good and bad fortune...They are skilled at creating and noticing chance opportunities, make lucky decisions by listening to their intuition, create self-fulfilling prophesies via positive expectations, and adopt a resilient attitude that transforms bad luck into good." Successful people essentially put luck in their favor through preparation and action. It's for this reason that Louis Pasteur, the French biologist and chemist, famously and accurately recognized that "chance favors only the prepared mind."

All this is to say you've got to prepare to succeed. Prepare to be more than average, to achieve more than the status quo, to be great, and to realize a compelling vision and big goals. Have great hope and instill hope in those around you, but make sure hope alone doesn't become your strategy for success and satisfaction.

Rule 19. Don't mistake a clear vision with a short distance.

Think about the vision you have and the big goals associated with that vision. We suspect it's something amazing, something insanely great, something desperately needed in the market. Perhaps it's a better mousetrap; maybe it's aiming for a personal best, a new product to overcome some frustration of a current product; or it could be something new that'll connect people in a deep and meaningful way. Whatever it is, the clearer your vision of it the better. You need to be able to convey the vision so that others see more than just your enthusiasm. They need to see real possibility and their work and purpose in that vision. They need to be able to share that vision with you and others as their own. It's equally important that you and those excited to journey with you understand that a clear vision, while great, is not likely synonymous with a short distance.

There's perhaps no better illustration of this than when President John F. Kennedy delivered his famous "We choose to go to the moon" speech at Rice Stadium in Houston, Texas. It was a hot September day in 1962 when he declared, "We choose to go to the moon in this decade and do the other things, not because they are easy, but because they are hard, because that goal will serve to organize and measure the best of our energies and skills, because that challenge is one that we are willing to accept, one we are unwilling to postpone." It was a clear vision but not a short distance.

Seven years after the speech, on July 20, 1969, *Apollo 11* landed the lunar module *Eagle* on the moon. The individuals involved certainly didn't mistake a clear vision with a short distance—as measured by time or space.

Our vision may not include intergalactic space exploration, but it will include goals. The thing about goals is that the clearer they are, the easier they are to communicate, and the easier they are to communicate, the easier they are to "see" as being possible. If you can get others to see your goals as clearly as you've envisioned them, it's easier for them to adopt them as their own.

The creator of the vision and those working to achieve it need to "see" the target—the ultimate vision and goals along the journey to reaching that vision. You see, sometimes, when the target or vision is too far away, or even out of sight, markers and guideposts need to be used as intermediate goals and as a tracking mechanism to measure both accuracy in alignment of work leading to the vision and cadence in progress of the work needed to accomplish the vision on time. Louie Ehrlich, a former president of information technology at Chevron, said, "We use aiming points." These aiming points break down a really big vision into more addressable feats of victory and success. For example, aiming points enable climbers to summit Mount Everest; they enable climbers to get from base camp to camp 1, then camp 2, then camp 3, then camp 4, which is referred to as the Death Zone, before reaching the summit nearly thirty thousand feet above sea level. On a high-visibility day, those trekking up the mountain can see the vision—the summit—clearly. But they know the clarity they have of their targeted vision isn't a short distance. Therefore, they need and use aiming points to set a path of realization to that vision.

Think about your vision. What aiming points do you have for yourself and your team? How are those aiming points helping to enable the realization of reaching that envisioned future state? To help ensure your success, cast a clear vision so that others see it as you do. Break it down into short-term goals and near-term wins with aiming points—monthly wins, weekly wins, and daily wins if possible.

You'll never achieve any vision in one fell swoop, but if you reach your aiming points with appropriate accuracy and cadence, you'll reach your bigger goals along the journey to ultimately achieving your vision.

Rule 20. If you're going to succeed, you've got to prioritize.

One key lesson to learn about goal setting is that it's an exercise in trade-offs and priorities. Each of our decisions is a trade-off of one thing over another or the timing of all things being considered.

You've probably heard something like this before: you can have anything, just not everything—or at least not everything all at once. You can have ice cream…but only after you eat your broccoli. This is a huge trade-off for a young person. The trades don't get any easier as you get older. There are financial trade-offs, career trade-offs, and many other life trade-offs. Whether you can explain opportunity cost in economic terms or not, we all can recognize that there are trade-offs involved in every decision we make. That's life. It's also a major function of leadership.

Life is a number of alternative decisions sacrificed. Every benefit is at the expense of a competing benefit. Understanding your priorities and trade-offs means understanding what you're *not* going to do. Michael Porter, a Harvard Business School professor and prolific author on strategy, said, "The essence of strategy is choosing what not to do."

Many organizations and people within organizations struggle with choosing, *period,* let alone being specifically intentional about what to do and, importantly, what *not* to do. It's easy to get bogged down by the decision or to take on too many things all at once and avoid the decision to choose at all. When you don't choose what not to do, you can find yourself adrift when it comes to your personal vision and confused when it comes to effectively establishing a position on anything. If you're not consciously choosing what to do and what not to do, you're likely open to try anything; worse yet, you might try to take on everything. That's no good. So make a decision—that's an important part of this rule and lesson. No vision is ever achieved when it's focused on everything.

The best leaders know their capacity to perform. Some know they can manage three priorities really well. For others, that number may be eight and for still others only two. What they also know is that when they take on one more than they can truly manage, it's not only the last one that suffers; rather, all the priorities they're trying to manage will suffer. John Marcante, the chief information officer at Vanguard, can shed a lot of light on effective leadership and achieving personal success and management of priorities. One of his guiding mantras is "I'd rather move three balls a mile than thirty balls an inch." Similarly, Jim Collins, author of *Good to Great* and *Great by Choice,* said, "If you have more than three priorities then you don't have any." This stands as a reminder of the importance of making trade-offs and managing priorities. If you're going to succeed, you've got to prioritize. If you're not consciously choosing what to do and what not to do, the three balls you should be focused on moving a mile likely will never get much farther than an inch.

What three balls must move a mile for your vision to be realized? Prioritize the three things you've got to absolutely get right. As you do, be sure to differentiate between the entire to-do list and the most important list. Follow the advice from Brian Engle, the executive director at the Retail Cyber Intelligence Sharing Center, who said, "Focus on the things that are most important, not just those things that you may be most equipped for. Lean into the challenges, especially those outside your comfort zone." This is a great reminder that sometimes we have to stop doing the things we are most comfortable doing so that we can start doing the things that matter the most.

We all know that our daily routine involves a number of tasks and activities that don't share the same level of priority. As you go about moving the three most important balls a mile, you may also want to heed the advice from Joshua Beeman, the executive director and information security officer at the University of Pennsylvania: "The main thing is keeping the main thing the main thing. Don't get distracted. Stay on point. Those who succeed are those who make incremental progress every day on the main thing." Devote your time, attention, energy, and strengths to your highest priorities and trade off all other efforts. In other words, focus on what matters the most, and ignore everything else.

Rule 21. Small details never are.

You may be familiar with, or at least have heard of, the book *Don't Sweat the Small Stuff* by Richard Carlson. Dr. Carlson further explains in the book's subtitle that *it's all small stuff*. Therein lies the challenge. It's all small stuff, and small details never are small, insignificant, or forgettable. Do you remember this old proverb?

> For want of a nail, the shoe was lost.
> For want of a shoe, the horse was lost.
> For want of a horse, the rider was lost.
> For want of a rider, the message was lost.
> For want of a message, the battle was lost.
> For want of a battle, the kingdom was lost.
> And all for the want of a horseshoe nail.

When it comes to details, the small ones never are small. All of them are important. Whether it be a product requirement, quality expectation, customer need, board member request, or part of a message to explain a vision, the details are important to ensuring results align with needs, goals, and strategy. So absolutely *sweat the small stuff*, because *it's all small stuff*.

Just as small actions are never small when trying to accomplish big goals, small details never are. In fact, it's often the small details that really thrill people enough to tell their friends, exert extra effort, and understand their role in something much bigger.

Harrison Barnes, the founder and chief executive officer of the Employment Research Institute, understands this rule. Not too long ago, he posted an article titled "Pay Attention to the Details." In it, he says, "One of the most important things you can do in your career, business, and life is pay attention to details." Indeed! He described the value and importance of details and concluded, "Where people win in business, in their careers, and elsewhere is often in the small print." Those are the details! Details always add up, just as the proverb above illustrates. The nail of a horseshoe can lose an entire kingdom. The best leaders communicate this importance to enable people to see the importance of their roles and responsibilities to the larger whole.

To further illustrate the power of small details, we want to introduce you to Mike, an academic friend of ours and former rocket scientist. Seriously, he worked for NASA, and according to his business card, he's a "rocket scientist."

Mike's job was to understand things like the dynamic load pressure relative to twin supersonic plume resonance and the implications from such pressure. He also researched the implications of Mach wave emission from supersonic jets operating at high temperatures and conducted a number of experiments to understand the impact that aeroacoustics friction at supersonic speeds had on aircraft material and the people inside. As we said, he's a rocket scientist!

The reason Mike is important here is his understanding of physics. To accomplish any big goal, you have to understand physics. Like us, you may not have an advanced degree in physics. Mike likely would say, "That's fine. Even without a degree in physics, you likely remember playing with dominoes as a kid." Again, if you're like us, your dominoes were all the same size and rectangular, and you enjoyed lining them up on end in a very even row (or perhaps with an occasional curve) before knocking one over and then watching the rest of them tumble one at a time when hit by the falling domino placed before it. That's physics!

The action and subsequent reaction of each domino is caused by mass in motion. The interesting thing about this is that, based on the mass and motion, a single domino can topple another that's 1.5 to 2 times its size in its path. That's important because your actions are similar, and you need them to be so to achieve any goal or desired future state. The reason why is because no goal of yours can be achieved in a single action. Any big goal is accomplished by aggregating small(er) accomplishments over time and aligned to the next larger one. In other words, big things are only accomplished one small detail at a time, added up over time.

Think back to when you were a kid playing with the dominoes. Think about the vision or end goal to see the last domino fall. Before that occurs, you need proper preparation, a strategy, and a plan for how the dominoes will be organized. You also need alignment to assure one domino's mass in motion will hit its next target and have the energy to topple it over and into the next domino. Every action of the domino will have a reaction. You have a similar effect as a leader. Your every action is affective—for better or worse. Whether you intend for it to affect or not, it does, and there's a subsequent effect. So act accordingly: prepare, plan, align, connect, and rely on your momentum (mass in motion) to accomplish smaller things that accumulate to much bigger things.

The best leaders look out for the details of the horseshoe nail. They know the kingdom relies on it, just as Mike knows of the catastrophic implications of a little friction at supersonic speed. You don't need to understand physics to be a great leader, but if you understand dominoes, you can appreciate and understand the need to sweat the small stuff.

Rule 22. Excellence is not an exception.

As you go about preparing to realize your vision, it's important to plan for excellence. Often—*too* often, actually—planning efforts are focused on "what" and not "how." Certainly, knowing *what* to do is vitally important if you have any chance of realizing the future state of a vision. But knowing *how* you will do it is even more important, because success is grounded in discipline. Planning the details of what will be done needs to be coupled with the way you and the team plan to get it done. Ideally, how you will do it is with an unparalleled level of excellence. Think about it: If not excellence, then what?

Excellence is preferred to any alternative, for sure. Excellence is the desired state for every individual and team, and it's realized through the discipline of executing details of a plan. This rule echoes rule 15: *don't fall into the temptation of mediocrity*, and *don't ease into the comfort of good enough!*

Perhaps the most consistent display of excellence is among the team of ladies and gentlemen at the Ritz-Carlton. They're known for their service excellence. Whether you've stayed at one of their hotels and experienced the level of their service firsthand or know of their service from others who have, you know they're the standard-bearer of excellence.

The most common understanding of excellence is being the best—the best quality; the best service; the best product; the best, period. Among teams today, leaders must drive excellence at the point of preparation so that it's an ingrained expectation throughout every action the team members take. You must drive excellence in the small things to realize excellence in all things. That's what makes the Ritz-Carlton team so renowned. They just get it because it's ingrained into them to do so. They prepare properly and have uncompromising follow-through.

It's important to note here that your sense of excellence mirrors how excellence is perceived by your customers, team members, and all other stakeholders. You see, excellence is similar to personal brand; it's important that you define it clearly so you understand it, but it's determined only from the perceptions of others.

Legendary football coach Vince Lombardi saw excellence as more than simply doing your best. He said, "The quality of a person's life is in direct proportion to their commitment to excellence, regardless of their chosen field of endeavor." How's your level of personal excellence? What level of excellence are you driving and realizing every day, with every action and every person? Are you delivering Ritz-Carlton levels of excellence in your work? If not excellence, then what?

Think about the immediate and downstream residual impact from delivering excellence in everything you do and everything your team does—not just for customers, but also for one another on the team and within the organization. Do you know the value of your excellence in service? Research from the American Society for Quality found that while 9 percent of customers will leave because they are lured away by the competition and 14 percent will leave because of dissatisfaction with a product, the vast majority—68 percent—will leave because of the experience they've had with one person. This is true with your customers and the level of excellence you should be focused on delivering. How's your collective level of excellence? Is it where you want to be, or are there improvements you need to make?

Don't sacrifice. Remember, your excellence is not an exception. It needs to be infused in the preparation of your work and in how you and your team go about work in everything and with everyone—every day.

Preparation: Reflect, Review, and Commit

- Do you have a strategy for the things you're trying to accomplish? If so, are there elements of your strategy that involve luck or chance or are based on hope alone? Consider how preparation and refined planning can decrease the variable of hope to create a more controlled outcome. With that in mind, what else can you do with strategy to increase the probability of achieving your goals?

- Think about a personal or professional goal. How can you break this goal into short-term goals and nearer-term wins? Now consider actionable steps. In light of your bigger goals, what are a few small actions you can take this month, this week, or even this day that'll move you toward your goal? Document a few aiming points that you might need to establish in order to make sure you're on track along the journey.

- Can you think of a time when an initiative didn't go the way you wanted it to because missing a small detail got in the way? How did you miss it? Consider an upcoming initiative that you want to see succeed. List and highlight a few small details that you need to get right to be successful.

- Considering the concept of moving three balls a mile versus thirty balls an inch, what are the three priorities you must move forward? Make the bold move to create a not-to-do list and document what you won't let get in the way of those priorities.

- Take a moment to determine what level of excellence you're delivering and realizing every day and with every action. How can you get better at building excellence into your planning efforts?

Action

Rule 23. Err on the side of action.

Leadership may be a noun as defined by traditional grammatical standards, but the best advice we've heard from great leaders is to treat your leadership as a verb. We hear time and again from leaders that while establishing a vision and conducting proper preparation are important efforts, they mean nothing if they're not followed by action.

A vision without action rots not only the vision but also the people who have a stake in that future state. Without action, people grow tired, frustrated, and cynical that anything can change the status quo, that any innovation can occur, that any greatness can be achieved, and that any vision can be realized. They lose trust in their leader and then in one another. A vision without action creates experiences that linger into the next vision and next plan; these negative experiences are often preconditions used to bet against realizing the new vision and plan by the same people who experienced inaction following the prior vision and plan. The cycle becomes perpetual for the next one, the one after that, the one after that, and so on—unless effective action disrupts the cycle.

Action can be hard because it's accompanied by risk and often occurs with less than full information. To be sure, there's a balancing act when it comes to visioning, thinking, planning, preparing, and taking action. No one wants to be stymied in analysis paralysis, nor does anyone want to move too far too fast. The challenge is striking a balance, but when in doubt, the most successful leaders say, "Err on the side of action!"

Your ability to execute is the key to achieving any goal. Regardless of clarity of vision or detailed preparation and strategy for success, without action, there's no progress. A bias toward action is a prerequisite for any success and is the number one reason for productivity. So as Bob Dethlefs, founder and chief executive officer of a number of successful organizations, told us, "Forego thy temptation to wait." When it comes to achieving success, realizing a big goal, or moving from status quo to something better, to start, just start!

This doesn't mean acting without proper preparation, with an ambiguous vision, with impulsivity, without foresight, or haphazardly. No, this is about having a direction and establishing movement—knowing that as you move, you can pivot your trajectory based on results and feedback you receive along the way; this is the basis of adaptive leadership. Move and keep moving. However small the action may be, take it, because as we learned from author and chief security officer Roland Cloutier, "Forward momentum, no matter how slight, is momentum," which can lead to much bigger gains. That's what you're looking to achieve. To start, just start. Then build momentum to sustain positive gains over time.

The best way to establish and maintain a bias toward action is to have a clear plan for the day, the week, the month, the quarter, the year, and so on. Obviously, the more you look into the future, the more uncertainty you'll face. So have clear lists for the day and the week, aiming points and deliverables for the month and the quarter, and higher level targets for the year and beyond. And at any point, when in doubt, err on the side of action, because the world is changed by what you *do*, not by your vision or preparation for what you *might* do.

Rule 24. You don't need unanimous consent to move forward.

We recognize that converting decisions into action can be difficult. Many strategies have emerged over the years in attempts to more effectively convert conversations to decisions and then convert decisions to action. There's the *majority rule* option. There's the *leave-it-to-the-executive-to-decide* option. *Consensus* is a popular option. There are serious issues with each of these strategies, but the one that causes the greatest challenge for leaders, especially inexperienced leaders, is thinking you need unanimous consent to move forward. You don't need unanimous consent to move from a conversation to a decision and, from there, to action.

While in a conversation with an executive at a very large, privately owned financial services firm, we learned this: "If you have a group of people that are 100 percent unanimous in any major—or even minor—decision, then one of two things is true: one, there are people in that group who are lying, or two, all of the people in that group are idiots."

What that executive described was essentially the Abilene Paradox. Jerry Harvey wrote a book called *The Abilene Paradox: The Management of Agreement,* and the following is the crux of the story:

> On a hot afternoon visiting in Coleman, Texas, a family is comfortably playing dominoes on a porch, until the father-in-law suggests that they take a trip to Abilene for dinner, which is 53 miles north of Coleman. The wife says, "Sounds like a great idea." The husband, despite having reservations because the drive is long and hot, thinks that his preferences must be out-of-step with the group and says, "Sounds good to me. I just hope your mother wants to go." The mother-in-law then says, "Of course I want to go. I haven't been to Abilene in a long time."

The drive is hot, dusty, and long. When they arrive at the cafeteria, the food is as bad as the drive. They arrive back home four hours later, exhausted.

One of them dishonestly says, "It was a great trip, wasn't it?" The mother-in-law says that, actually, she would rather have stayed home, but went along since the other three were so enthusiastic. The husband says, "I wasn't delighted to be doing what we were doing. I only went to satisfy the rest of you." The wife says, "I just went along to keep you happy. I would have had to be crazy to want to go out in the heat like that." The father-in-law then says that he only suggested it because he thought the others might be bored.

The group sits back, perplexed that they together decided to take a trip which none of them wanted. They each would have preferred to sit comfortably, but did not admit to it when they still had time to enjoy the afternoon.

Reaching unanimous consent—or even general consensus, for that matter—requires a group of people to reach an agreement. Most people think it's the leader's role to get everyone in agreement. Unfortunately, in many attempts to reach an agreement, the Abilene Paradox becomes present. No one wants to "rock the boat," so to speak, but when you find yourself and your team in Abilene, it's a clear indication of the leader's inability to manage the agreement—or more importantly, the decision.

Liane Davey, the psychologist and business strategist, offered critical advice to all leaders in her *Harvard Business Review* article: "If your team agrees on everything, working together is pointless." Unanimous consent isn't needed to make decisions. In fact, it rarely, if ever, truly exists among a team. If it does, you should immediately wonder who may be lying, who simply doesn't want to rock the boat, and worse yet, who's on the team but just doesn't care about the team or the work they're doing together. If you proceed without questioning the consensus, you're fooling yourself about the decision and very likely are on your way to Abilene.

The reality is that you'll never have complete consensus on any topic of importance. With that in mind, it's not as important to get unanimous consent as it is to make decisions, move to action, and start building positive momentum. The best leaders create conditions and cultures in which participants can disagree but then commit to action. Be a great leader by driving conversations that lead to decisions that are followed by immediate action.

Rule 25. Don't confuse effort with progress or output with outcomes.

How often do you greet people throughout the day and ask, "How's it going?" or "What are you working on?" Probably a lot. How often do you get an immediate response such as, "Wow, there's a lot going on," or "We're really busy working on a lot of things today?" Is the response one of effort or progress? It's easy to be busy, and it's good to be busy. Output is important. But it's far better to make *progress* on a major *outcome*. So yes, busy is good, but productive is much better. Effective leaders ensure their team is producing outcomes and not mired in busywork

Effectiveness and success are about progress, not effort. They're about outcome, not output. Now some people view output and outcome as mere semantics, and that's unfortunate—the differences are much more profound than semantics alone. An outcome is something your customers, clients, and employees can actually see and experience. These are results, and they serve as a measure of performance—not just effort, but performance. Anyone or any team of people in your company may very well be busy working on a number of things, but that busyness doesn't assure an effective outcome. It's for this reason that the best leaders focus on outcomes rather than outputs.

Bob Behn, a lecturer at Harvard's John F. Kennedy School of Government, said, "The only thing that counts is an outcome. The only thing worth counting is an outcome." We agree. In a time of gross self-aggrandizing efforts, busyness, and a wide sense of self-entitlement, our reality is that no one really cares how hard you work. You're expected to work hard, but working hard doesn't guarantee your success. Outcome trumps output, accomplishment trumps effort, value actions trump value statements, and results trump any level of intent.

Let's think about output versus outcome through the lens of products. There's no arguing that McDonald's has sold a lot of hamburgers over the years. It's been calculated (and posted in marketplace.org) that they sell about seventy-five burgers every second. That's well over two billion burgers sold in a year. According to the NPD Group's food-service market research, there are about nine billion burgers sold and consumed every year. So while McDonald's sells the most by far, consumers do have options. Besides McDonald's, we can buy burgers from In-N-Out Burger, Five Guys, Shake Shack, and Red Robin, to name a few. But let's get back to outputs versus outcomes. Selling more burgers is an output, not an outcome. Shake Shack doesn't want to be compared to McDonald's, and while they may be happy with selling more burgers, they're focused on something even more important to them: the consumer's experience. Their desired outcome is a positive customer experience and they believe that outcome occurs from using better ingredients, providing better service, and perhaps offering a better environment. Certainly you'll pay for that difference. Shake Shack burgers are more expensive than a burger at McDonald's. You can buy a hamburger from McDonald's for about a dollar. It'll cost at least three times that amount at the other restaurants mentioned. But what are they creating? What's the outcome? It's not about the number of burgers sold but rather the customer's experience.

Outcome isn't about making or selling more stuff. That's output. Outcome is the impact you have on customers. It's much more aligned with the vision of the future state. It's the reason Maserati isn't focused on catching Volkswagen to be the number one seller of automobiles. Maserati isn't focused on that output. Rather, their vision and focus are on creating the best user experience for their buyers, drivers of high-performance automobiles.

This experience isn't just limited to consumers. It's applicable to employees as well. Think about the outcomes you're aiming to provide your customers. The only way they'll experience what you have envisioned is through interaction with your employees—the products and services they provide. With that in mind, what interactions do you have with your employees? What experiences are you providing them? What outcomes do you want your employees to have so that, in turn, they'll create the outcomes you have planned for your costumers? All of your actions matter because you're always influencing those around you. You're either enabling those around you to be great or inhibiting them from being so. If you're intentionally creating experiences for your employees to be great and do great work, that'll lead to higher levels of engagement and customer service from them, which will lead to better outcomes all around.

As a parting note here, we do realize that outputs are important for managers within organizations. They'll likely always be measured. The importance of this rule, however, is that while outputs may provide some perspective about the busyness of your business, don't allow the focus on outputs to blind you to the importance of your outcomes. The best leaders align outcomes to their vision and understand (and measure) the outcomes they intend to realize among their team, across the enterprise, with their products and services, and with their customers and clients.

Rule 26. Don't get your actions ahead of your culture's readiness to act.

Aristotle said, "Change in all things is sweet." From some perspectives, that may be true, but if you've ever experienced periods of big transformation or massive and disruptive change, you may very well take issue with Aristotle's fervor in explaining it with such palatability.

In business and in life, even change brought about by a leader with a clear vision and proper planning can be fraught with risk and challenge. It's for this reason that most efforts to bring about a new order of things fail. The odds of success are usually worse than the odds of failure. As David Pottruck, a former chief executive officer at Charles Schwab, said, when it comes to change, "the deck is stacked against you."

Regardless of the odds, most actions you take as a leader are in an effort to change the status quo to something better. This effort is necessary for anyone or any team, organization, or community hoping to keep pace in an increasingly competitive and complex world that is constantly changing. Nothing and no one survives, let alone realizes mild achievement or especially great success, without vision, preparation, and action to change. Business author Alan Deutschman reminded us of this fact, noting our option to either "Change or Die," which was the title of his *FastCompany* article. Grim...but true.

While you may think your organization—and the people within it—could change when it matters most, Deutschman warns that "you're probably deluding yourself." Decades of research confirm that only a small handful of change efforts are ever truly successful. If individual and cultural resistances to change are greater than the compelling vision of the future and how to get there, the change will fail. The truth is, if there's limited dissatisfaction in the current state of things, lackluster vision of a possible future state, and ambiguous or overly zealous steps to get there, cultural and human resistance will overcome the effort to realize the envisioned change every time.

In addition to making sure there's sufficient dissatisfaction in the current state, clarity in the vision of the future state, and proper preparation in the planned steps to get there, leaders can also increase their probability of success by ensuring their actions don't outpace the readiness of their teams or enterprise of employees. Because any effort to realize a vision likely requires people to operate on the fringe of their capability and bring about new ways of performance and behaving, the best leaders know not to go too far beyond that fringe too quickly; otherwise, they end up in the fear zone, which will fuel resistance and freeze action.

As you go about any aspect of change, you've got to make sure the path of change is aligned with a readiness to change. Any time you get change ahead of your employees' readiness, you're going to have problems. So be aware of the current state of change readiness, and don't get your actions to bring about some change ahead of the employees' readiness to act in support of that change.

Rule 27. However bad you think it is, it's not as bad as you think.

As we've mentioned, when setting out on a course of action in an attempt to realize a big vision, you'll certainly encounter risks and challenges. You'll also need to face some fears along the journey. No doubt you'll have some bad days that'll put you under pressure, and you may not act in a way for which you've prepared or in a way you desire. In fact, you may act irrationally. Most irrationality is based on either fatigue, mental or physical, or bias due to misperception or a blind spot. When we encounter either, we see current situations and forecast future possibilities through an exaggerated lens of reasoning. It's at these times that anxiety can spike. Poor reasoning follows, and then poor judgment sets in.

This is often followed by poor decisions and actions, and before you know it, compounding effects start to ripple in increasing magnitude, affecting not only you but those around you.

The best leaders learn to avoid the trap of irrationality when facing challenges by focusing on what's referred to as the "long view." The long view is simply the ability to maintain focus on long-term goals and objectives. So when these leaders encounter challenges, they think in terms of what effects those challenges will have in the future, not in the present. Even though a situation may seem dire and creates a high level of stress in the present, by thinking of the realistic, long-term impact, you have the opportunity to realize that things may not be as bad as you currently perceive them to be.

One of the authors of this book, who at times shares a story while teaching or lecturing about his worst day at work, learned this lesson. While managing a project funded by the US government, he one day found himself in front of a group of senators who were none too pleased that his project was significantly behind schedule. With emotions running high and a focus on the immediate challenges, irrational behavior and comments filled the day. Unfortunately, the people in the room lost focus on the fact that great work was being done that had never been done before and that the strategic benefits of the project were significant, regardless of the current loss of schedule. In the long term, the project turned out to be highly successful, the senators were pleased, and the short-term problems encountered along the journey didn't seem so dire in the end.

In addition to the long-view tactic, a wonderful and simple technique for getting past short-term challenges is offered by Colin Powell. His technique? Sleep on it. As he advises, "It ain't as bad as you think. It'll look better in the morning." Now General Powell is quick to note that things may *not* actually be better in the morning. He's not offering a prediction; rather, he's making the point that stepping away from the urgency of a challenge for a period of time and giving your mind a rest may shed new light on possible solutions and provide an opportunity to reset perspective from a short to a long view.

So if you feel yourself being persuaded by emotional irrationality rather than good, sound judgment, remind yourself that the situation is likely not as bad as your exaggeration is making it. If possible, step away and take a fresh look at the situation in the light of a new day.

Rule 28. Play both defense and offense.

We grew up immersed in sports of all kinds and maybe because of that find ourselves thinking in sporting analogies from time to time. This leadership rule may be easiest to think about and understand through the lens of a sports analogy.

If you played a sport, you likely learned very quickly that most sports contain an aspect of both offense and defense. And in some sports, there are actually separate units for offense and defense: the players play either offense or defense, not both. You'll hear sports commentators talk about teams or coaches who focus more on either offense or defense. They'll use expressions such as "play to your strengths," "defense wins championships," or "you're going to have to outscore your opponent." All are commonplace in sports situations and communications.

In leadership, you don't get the choice of focusing your preparation and actions on either offense or defense. You've got to learn how to do both. To be great, you've got to practice both. There are situations where you must go to bat for your team. Nothing builds respect and a loyal following better. There are times when you're going to need to take big risks and face your fears in order to go after what's in front of you. You're going to need to show up and work hard to forge ahead even when you don't feel like it.

Additionally, you'll need to survey the competition and look for areas of opportunities—learn how to leverage your strengths or exploit your opponent's weaknesses.

All of those scenarios are focused on offense, but there are moments of defense, too. Excellent leaders shelter their teams from their own frustrations. They protect their teams from situations they don't need to know about or be involved in. They don't allow their own bad days to affect their teams' actions as they work to accomplish big things. The best leaders know how to be conflict managers and remove people from conflict when the results are going to be damaging. They take responsibility for their actions and their teams' actions and ultimately assume responsibility for their teams' successes and failures. The best leaders don't ask their teams to do anything they wouldn't be willing to do themselves.

So in sports, there will be players who specialize in shot blocking or covering the other team's best player (defensive specialists), and there will be others who have a sole focus on throwing, shooting, or kicking (offensive specialists). Leaders aren't afforded an either-or option. While you may have strengths in one or the other, as a leader you've got to play both defense and offense to realize your vision and enable your team to win.

Rule 29. Measure what matters—only what matters.

If you're going to focus on action in an effort to accomplish something, anything, you're going to want to measure it. How else will you know if you're making progress, getting better, achieving what's possible, and staying on track to reach your aiming points and realize your envisioned future state?

You've got to be careful, though, as you go about making sense of your work by using metrics and measures. Russ Martinelli, Jim Waddell, and Tim Rahschulte wrote the book *Program Management for Improved Business Results*. In it, they note, "Metrics are powerful;

or perhaps more precise, *for better or worse*, metrics are powerful. Metrics are part of a larger organizational construct—the performance management system—and if not used properly, they can do as much harm as good. Hence, the 'for better or worse' caveat."

You see, measuring in and of itself isn't hard. To measure, you've got to have data, and in today's data age, that's not a problem. There's more data available to us today than ever before, and its availability is growing. So accessing data isn't the problem. Interpreting data, on the other hand, can get real tricky, real fast.

The goal with data and the use of metrics is to make sense of what's happening and forecast what's next. Or as we've heard from some leaders over the years, you've got to "collect the dots and then connect the dots." You need to understand all of what's going on, make sense of what's going on, and figure out how it all affects your business goals and vision. You want to be able to use data to gain clarity and insights regarding what's currently happening based on actions taking place and what may happen because of the actions and resultant outputs and outcomes. In his article "The ABCs of Analytics," David Meer, a partner at Booz Allen, wrote, "Any analysis of data that stops after asking 'what,' which is already a big undertaking, isn't analytics. You have to ask 'why?' and 'what next?'" Connecting the dots for intelligence helps to understand what's next for decision making and the actions that follow.

When it comes to true insights and intelligence, however, most organizations struggle. They either try to measure too much, measure the wrong things, measure without specific cadence, or measure to create bureaucracy—the list goes on, and none of it creates clarity, let alone intelligence. Instead, it actually creates confusion, frustration, and disengagement from action.

Just because data are easy to collect doesn't mean they're useful. Remember rule 25: *don't confuse effort with progress or output with outcomes.* You've got to measure what matters most.

Performance management isn't about finding the "perfect" metrics to measure and manage. Perfect metrics don't exist. Find the measures and metrics that explain your business—those you can use to tell a story and make decisions that lead you to your next aiming point and critical outcome. The best metrics are simple, with data that are easily accessible, understandable, and consistently useable.

It's common knowledge that what gets measured gets managed and what gets managed is most likely to improve over time. Anything we do and anything we think is worth doing is also worth measuring. We were reminded of this by Partha Srinivasa, the chief information officer at HCC Insurance Holdings Inc., who said, "If you don't measure it, it doesn't exist." But you've got to collect the right data to measure the right things for any improvement to be realized. Instead of getting access to more data, the most relevant question for most of us is what we should measure. You and everyone on your team should know the answer to that question.

To know what to measure, you have to know what's important. Don't confuse important things with just those things that you value. Things you value may be important, but they may not be. The things to measure are those relative to critical outcomes and those that prove assurance that you're aligned with your aiming points and vision. To understand these metrics and measures means that you may need to ask others who are across the enterprise what's most important for them relative to working toward your joint purpose and vision. Many leaders say, "I measure what you treasure." This is an often-used phrase and one Tom Schuman wrote about in his article "Measure What You Treasure." It's good advice. It encourages us to look beyond what we value to the interests of those we're reporting to and serving through our actions. Learn what matters most to them. Learn the business through the perspective of others. Measure what they treasure. Measure what matters most.

Rule 30. Don't let yesterday's frustrations hijack today's successes.

Along any journey, we'll make mistakes. We'll make improper decisions and have illogical actions. It's been said that these missteps in our past—our past actions—cannot be erased. That's true and simply means that the consequences of your actions never leave you. They're part of your path and journey. Past actions, however, aren't there to haunt us, taunt us, or keep us from achieving our goals, dreams, aspirations, and visions of future states—although they may seem to do so from time to time. It's best to keep in mind that our past actions have occurred; therefore, they're in the past—not the present and not the future.

You're probably familiar with some of the more remarkable stories of individuals who have turned life's missteps and setbacks into amazing success stories. Here are a few classic examples that you may have already heard: Steve Jobs was fired from his position at Apple; Bill Gates's first company went under; Michael Jordan was cut from his high school basketball team; Abraham Lincoln lost eight elections and experienced a nervous breakdown; J. K. Rowling at one point was unemployed and described herself as a big failure; Oprah Winfrey was fired from her first television position; and even Henry Ford failed multiple times, which resulted in personal bankruptcies. There are many other stories, and you likely have your own, where actions and circumstances caused negative outcomes and missteps along a journey that likely was well-intentioned, properly prepared, and void of any thought of challenge or setback.

We know you're likely thinking it's easy to be inspired by others who have turned failure into success, but it can be much more difficult to move past our own failures and frustrations. We're inspired by such stories because we get to see the end. We know and remember the successes of others because of their success. We don't always remember the struggles they faced, the fear they had to overcome, and their actions that followed a downfall. However, when it comes to our own frustrations, setbacks, and missteps, we can easily allow them to hijack future success because we lack the ability to see a positive outcome that awaits us.

To prevent the past from hijacking the present, we need to realize where it is—it's behind us! If you need to start over, start now.

Experiences from the past can fuel us to succeed today...but only if we can cope with any past setback rather than having it devalue our self-efficacy, damage our self-determination, prevent us from reaching our planned achievements, and consume us with fear to the point of inaction. When it comes to the setbacks in the past, cope with them, deal with them, and learn from them. Then let them go and focus on action. Focus on your immediate next step along your journey. Remember, success isn't limited to a select few. It's available to anyone willing to have a vision, prepare properly, follow through with actions, and overcome hurdles, missteps, and setbacks.

Our experiences are all in the past. They shape who we are, but they don't determine who we will be. They illustrate what we've accomplished but not our vision of what's next. They harbor the consequences of our missteps but not our potential. Only from present activities do we determine who we are and who we will become, what we are willing to do, and what we will achieve. So even if you've had some bad experiences or missed achieving a goal (or many goals), it's okay. Get better today. And then get even better tomorrow. And then repeat. Err on the side of action, or risk having yesterday's frustrations hijack your potential for success today.

Rule 31. Did I do my absolute best today?

The last few rules have been focused on measuring your action for effectiveness. This should be a daily reflection activity to ensure we're showing up in the right way and doing our very best every day. If you've seen the movie *Facing the Giants*, you're likely familiar with this philosophy and rule. The movie is about an underdog high school football team and a coach trying to send a powerful message about leadership: do your best, your very best, your absolute best.

The leader among the players in the movie is Brock. What he says, the players believe, and what he does, they mimic. In one scene, on the practice field, Brock's teammate raises a question about how strong an upcoming opponent is that year. Before the coach can reply, Brock says, "A lot stronger than we are."

The coach fires back, "You already written Friday night down as a loss, Brock?"

Brock replies, "Well, not if I know we could beat them." The coach takes this as an opportunity for Brock to focus on his best, his very best, his absolute best, and to show his leadership capabilities and responsibilities to the rest of the team.

The coach asks Brock to do the "death crawl." Now, for those of you unfamiliar with high school football practices, routines, and workouts, the death crawl is an exercise in which someone carries another person on his back while crawling on his hands and feet, without any other part of his body touching the ground. Not easy! Going twenty or thirty yards would be good.

Brock asks the coach how far he needs to go. He thinks he can carry his teammate on his back while doing the death crawl from the end zone to the thirty-yard line. The coach believes Brock can go much farther and asks Brock to simply "give your best, your very best, your absolute best." Brock agrees.

To make sure Brock's psychological fatigue doesn't get the best of him at the thirty-yard line and falsely proclaim victory, the coach blindfolds him. Brock sets off from the end zone with his teammate, Jeremy, on his back. His coach is alongside him every yard of the crawl. His coach encourages him. "You gotta keep moving.

Let's keep moving. Let's go. Don't quit till you got nothing left. There you go. Keep moving."

After doing the death crawl for a while, Brock replies, "It hurts...he's heavy."

"I know it hurts," the coach replies. "You keep going. It's not hard from here. Thirty more steps. You keep going, Brock. Come on. Keep going."

Brock thinks he's gone way past the thirty-yard line. "That's gotta be fifty. That's gotta be fifty. I don't have any more." The coach encourages him to focus on the work and not to worry about the yard line. He encourages Brock to focus on giving his very best.

When Brock loses the strength to crawl any farther, he falls to the ground. He thinks he's made it to at least the fifty-yard line. "That's gotta be fifty. That's gotta be fifty," Brock says, exhausted. It was actually much farther. He went a hundred yards, and the coach lets him know. "You're in the end zone, Brock."

And then the coach gives the lesson: "Brock, you are the most influential player on this team. If you walk around defeated, so will they. Now tell me you can't give me more than what I've been seeing." Perhaps more importantly, he reminds Brock that he's a leader and needs to think about his leadership. "Don't waste it." Then he asks, "Can I count on you?"

Brock replies, "Yes."

At this point, Brock realizes he can accomplish much more than he thinks. The same is likely true for you, us, everyone. Think about your day and your actions throughout it. Are you doing your best, your very best, your absolute best? Do you want to stop at the thirty-yard line although your potential is another seventy beyond that? It's something to reflect on every day.

Don't sell yourself short. Don't rely on small goals. And remember that you're always being watched. People are looking to you and following you. They're taking your lead as a leader. If you're not giving your best, no one else will either. Be a leader. Give your best, your very best, your absolute best every day, all day.

Abraham Lincoln said, "I do the very best I know how, the very best I can, and I mean to keep on doing so until the end." This rule was clearly part of his leadership philosophy, perspective, and style. If you're looking for a daily checklist or reminder of this rule, Marshall Goldsmith has outlined six questions that, when used every day, will make you better and increase the probability of successfully realizing your future-state vision. Here are the questions:

- Did I do my best to set clear goals?
- Did I do my best to be fully engaged?
- Did I do my best to make progress toward goal achievement?
- Did I do my best to build positive relationships?
- Did I do my best to find meaning?
- Did I do my best to be happy?

Those are six great questions to reflect on daily to ensure your actions leverage your preparation and align to your vision. Each of these questions is personal. It's not by accident that each one starts with "Did I do my best." Being our best isn't about waiting for someone else. It's an individual responsibility and the reason the questions don't ask if my coach or teacher helped me do my best. It's good when others help us, but it's our responsibility to own our actions and to show up prepared to do our best and follow through on that preparation. That's the reason to ask whether you've done your absolute best.

Action: Reflect, Review, and Commit

- What's something you've been meaning to get around to but just haven't done yet? How would things look different if you just did it?
- Is there a frustration or personal failure that's holding you back? What is it? What have you learned from it? Commit here to the lessons learned while simultaneously letting go and moving forward.
- Do you find yourself seeking full consensus in decision making? How might this be interfering with your ability to make maximum progress? Document at least one current decision where you can go about seeking commitment without the need for unanimous consent.
- Where might you be confusing effort with progress or output with outcomes? How might you most clearly label your key outcomes? What are you measuring to verify if you're on track and making progress? How do these measures align with what's most important?
- What's a challenge that you're currently facing where a fresh perspective could be helpful? How can you get some distance from the situation to reestablish a new outlook? Are there some trusted individuals you could consult with to help you see the situation more clearly? Schedule time with them, get a new perspective, and set a long view.
- Think about a personal or professional change that you're in the midst of or have coming up. Who's going to need to be part of that change to make it successful? Have you assessed their readiness for this effort? Consider what you can do now to give yourself a better chance of success by aligning the pace of change with individual readiness.

- Be honest with yourself. Have you given your very best today, this week, this month? Where can you see opportunity for personal improvement by giving more? In what areas of your life have you settled for something less than what you're capable of? Can you reset your preparation, and what shows up when you do to assure that you're giving your absolute best?

Section 2: Station Break

Challenging the status quo can be difficult. It could mean going in a different direction from a predecessor or challenging cultural legacy that's been immovable for years (or even much longer). Don't be afraid to do things differently. Have the courage to push the boundaries of where you are to where you want to be—where you need to be or where you and your team can be.

Speaking of where you can be, at this point, you can likely find yourself at the Minot, North Dakota, station stop along your journey from Seattle to Chicago. Or maybe you've made it just beyond Minot to the Rugby station stop. If so, you're near the county seat of Pierce County, North Dakota, which is the geographical center of North America.

There's no better place than the center of the continent to think about the pillars upon the foundation of your leadership: vision, preparation, and action. Pause, reflect, and talk with your friends, neighbors, colleagues, and other leaders about where you are and where you're going.

Section 2 covered seventeen rules of great leaders and leadership. These rules on vision, preparation, and action really help you to center your focus on what needs to be done and how it can be done. While your leadership potential may be grounded in your mindset, purpose, and perspective (section 1), that potential is realized only if and when you have a clear vision, proper preparation, and a bias toward action. These are the three enabling factors that support all that happens from your engagement as a leader.

Spend some time here to truly understand the pillars of your leadership, because only from understanding them will you be able to conceptualize what's possible because of you. While you think about the last seventeen rules, consider the following:

- Which rules in this section really resonated with you? How do you intend to put them into practice in the near future?
- Which rules of your own might you add to this section? How are they relevant to where you are right now?

Your success as a leader requires the strength and efficacy of a strong foundation—your mindset, purpose, and perspective—but that alone won't guarantee your success. The pillars of your leadership—your vision, preparation, and action—are necessary for you and your team to succeed. That's been the focus of this station break.

Section 3
The People Practices of Great Leaders and Leadership

Leadership is about leaders and followers working together in a joint effort connected by a common purpose to reach the vision of a desired future state. Based on this relationship, leaders and followers need one another. If there are no followers, there's certainly no leader—nor is there any need for leadership. If there's no leader, there will be stifled progress at best, regardless of the number of able followers. Without a leader, followers drift ambiguously, and a leader without anyone following is not a leader at all. In short, leadership is all about people. It's about leaders who cast a future vision of success, and it's about followers who enable that success.

To be a great leader, you can't ignore the human connection of leadership itself or the human complexities involved with leading. The best leaders address such connections and complexities by establishing a common purpose, vision, and collaboration needed to enable the possible future state to be realized. This is what followers need from a leader. They need to be inspired, encouraged, recognized, believed in, and challenged to accomplish a meaningful purpose and vision. Because of this, leadership is important.

The foundation of leadership is the core of any leader's capability. The pillars of leadership that rise up from that foundation strengthen it and further enable the leader's capability. But it's from engagement and interactions with people that the leader drives attitude and performance, and is ultimately the measure of the leader's success, effectiveness, and legacy. That's the focus of the eighteen rules divided across *people leadership*, *team leadership*, and *self-leadership* in section 3.

People Leadership

Rule 32.	Make it personal.
Rule 33.	Control things, manage processes, and lead people.
Rule 34.	Work with people from where they are.

Rule 35.   Don't try to be a friend; rather, be a friendly leader.

Rule 36.   Learn from others and pass it on.

Team Leadership

Rule 37.   Wearing a uniform doesn't make a team.

Rule 38.   Nobody's bigger than the team.

Rule 39.   Never walk past a mistake.

Rule 40.   Don't confuse being right with getting it right.

Rule 41.   Find a way to say yes.

Rule 42.   When it comes to engagement, you won't get everyone.

Rule 43.   You're not your team, but you're defined by your team.

Rule 44.   Your success is a social journey.

Self-Leadership

Rule 45.   Life's not fair; get used to it.

Rule 46.   You can't control your situation, but you can control your choice.

Rule 47.   You bring your weather.

Rule 48.   You can't wait to be great.

Rule 49.   You're leading and leaving a legacy; act accordingly.

Success doesn't simply happen because of a clear vision of what's possible and proper preparation for carrying out a plan. Rather, it's from the work among people who enable that vision to be realized. Therefore, while a leader may envision what's possible and prepare the route to get there, people are the drivers of success. The leader's responsibility is to harmonize people's work in a way that ensures the capacity of what's possible among them is greater than that from any separate part of the team or individual. To do this effectively, the leader must make the connection between people and purpose personal. This means much more than offering an inspirational speech or showing up in a charismatic way. Although these things can be important, this is really about extending the meaning of the team's work, helping each member of the team get better personally, and helping the team get better collectively. And, since each person on any team is an individual, this requires the leader to display individualized consideration. This should come as no surprise. People are unique, and a one-size-fits-all approach doesn't work. A singular approach isn't useful in all situations or even for individuals experiencing the same situation. People leadership is personal. This means the leader must know and understand members of the team, their strengths, and what they're aiming to accomplish. This understanding is needed for the leader to meet people where they are in terms of capability, capacity, and potential before assuming expectations for where they need to be in order to realize the team's purpose. Meeting people where they are is needed for action as well as learning and development, because personal growth doesn't occur far beyond one's current capacity; rather, it's on the fringe of what's already known and possible. Leaders work on this fringe to extend individual capability, which then also extends a team's collective capacity to perform.

Any individual capability is nominal relative to what a team of individuals can accomplish together. But it takes a lot more than a uniform or logo to make a group of individuals function as a team. It takes effective team leadership to establish collaboration and care between individuals, the willingness to support one another, the commitment to one another, and the desire to see one another succeed without jealousy, envy, or spite. Leaders enable this by ensuring no one is bigger than the team, including the leader. The best teams focus on getting it right over any one person being right. This type of culture increases individual engagement but certainly won't create full engagement. The best leaders know that aiming for full engagement is foolish, but while it doesn't stop them from trying, it doesn't stymie them from taking action and making progress either. They know full engagement isn't needed to make progress. They progress by using many other tactics, including saying yes as often as possible and resolving "either-or" arguments with "both-and" solutions.

Importantly, while the best leaders are aware and knowledgeable of each person and their team, they are also self-aware. They know they don't define their effectiveness. That conclusion is determined by their followers. They do know, however, that they influence how their effectiveness is perceived: it's by the choices they make. Just as you choose to live your life, the way you lead is a choice. Leaders, like all of us, make choices regarding how they show up every day, whether their attitude is good or bad, optimistic or pessimistic, full of possibility or drowning in limitations. As a leader, you can't wait to be great. You have to choose to be great now. The best leaders realize that their every action—e-mail, phone call, hallway conversation—leaves an impression on others and on their legacy as a leader. Knowing this, act accordingly—not as if leadership is a bolt-on task but rather an integrated behavior.

Before reading the eighteen rules of *people leadership, team leadership,* and *self-leadership* in this section, pause to think about your leadership. Is it a bolt-on task used periodically based on convenience or an integrated behavior that shows up always? Consider these questions and your legacy as you build upon the foundation of leadership rules from section 1 and the pillars of leadership rules from section 2.

People Leadership

Rule 32. Make it personal.

Remember, it's all about people. It's not strategies or policies, processes or plans—it's people who produce results. Organizations can have the most detailed and elaborate strategies acutely aligned with organizational capacity and based on an extremely precise customer analysis that includes the most attractive acquisition tactics and go-to-market plans for any product or service offering, but without competent and engaged people, the organization will fall short of its possibilities, or worse, it may fail completely. Anything you set out to do, accomplish, or change is about people. It's all about people. The best leaders know this and focus their time on—you guessed it—people.

The best leaders focus their efforts on developing people, coaching people, aligning their work, and supporting them. Many times, however, even capable leaders lose sight of the importance of people. Sometimes we think about people in terms of units or as economic variables to be used rather than a "human" resource to be elevated. As we were reminded by Roland Cloutier, the chief security officer and author, "Alignment drives connection and the way you get things done is through human connection." In order to achieve this level of reality, the leader must make work personal. There are a number of ways to go about this, but any leader who has had any success knows that the number one priority as a leader is to take care of your people: inspire them to do great work and help them to be great, period. To do so, you'll need to rely on one very critical capability: you'll need to care.

Only if you care can you make it personal. You'll need to care about the mission of the company, for sure. But more importantly, you'll need to care about the individuals in the company trying to make that mission mean something even more. You'll need to help people understand the meaning and value of their work. Work without meaning is also without care, without heart, without soul, and without purpose.

Great leaders recognize that there's more to work than simply getting it done. They connect that work to the person and the person to the larger meaning of the whole product. They create a line of sight from what's being done individually to the vision collectively and, in so doing, create clarity in one's potential, impact, and value.

It's important to note here that in many cases, the greatest needs and moments people have are outside of work. The best leaders realize that people are employees eight hours a day but people twenty-four hours a day. These leaders care about the whole person, not just a third of the whole person or some other fraction. They act as if everyone is important at all times, because they are. And as we were reminded by Amber Case, the author of *Cyborg Anthropology*, a fellow at Harvard University's Berkman Klein Center for Internet and Society, and a visiting researcher at MIT, they treat people the way they want them to become. As she explained, "People become the people you treat them to be." You make work personal, and people start taking it personally, which deepens the meaning of their work, aligns them more purely to the mission, and increases their engagement. That's what the best leaders do. They make it personal, and they take ownership of that responsibility.

Rule 33. Control things, manage processes, and lead people.

In *The Principles of Scientific Management,* Frederick Winslow Taylor wrote, "The principal object of management should be to secure the maximum prosperity for the employer, coupled with the maximum prosperity for each employee." Prosperity, as he defined it, was about higher wages and, importantly, the development of each employee to his or her optimal state of possibility.

Taylor was certainly looking to optimize the efficiency of the company, but he was also outlining the need for leaders to look out for the benefit of their employees—to care about them, their families, and their livelihoods. Taylor thought the best way to do this was to first illustrate the inefficiencies in our daily routines of work and to next convince people that the remedy for such inefficiencies is scientific and systematic management of processes and functions in our routines.

Taylor realized then, in 1911, the difference between leadership and management. The latter is grounded in science and focused on continual improvement through efficiency. The former is an art of influence that's effective only through the personal connection with people and their desire of work—both the value of the company's outcome from each individual's effort and the value as seen beyond the employee to its effect on family, friends, and community. The importance of this was echoed by Cynthia Trudell, the chief human resources officer at PepsiCo, who said, "You control things, you manage processes, and you lead people." That's true!

You don't work with people the same way you would leverage a process or use a tool or any other "thing" for that matter. You work with people—especially when leading them—to make a connection between the person and the work being performed and from one person to another throughout the organization and beyond. It's about making meaningful contact and experiences, and doing so with an understanding that the whole person is important.

Remember, a person is an employee for just a third of any given day.

For many employees, leaders know that connecting the person, the work, and meaning sometimes means looking beyond the work itself—understanding and helping to support the person's nonwork life. This is often a stumbling block for struggling leaders, but in understanding this, a leader finds the "true" power to lead, which is to care, connect, and realize the whole person.

Rule 34. Work with people from where they are.

Do you remember the relationship between Mr. Miyagi and Daniel in the movie *The Karate Kid?* Daniel is being bullied and needs to face his rival, Johnny Lawrence from the Cobra Kai Dojo, in a local karate tournament. He looks to Mr. Miyagi, the maintenance man for the apartment complex where Daniel and his mom live, to train him. Instead of training Daniel based on "best practices" or the technique of the modern day, Mr. Miyagi orients his process around Daniel. He seeks first to know him and then to determine the methods that will work best given what he finds. Daniel ends up learning as much about life as he does about karate. The best coaches can have that kind of effect. They consider the individual capacity of their team before determining specific approaches for development. They coach at an individual level, knowing that each person is unique.

We all work to accomplish things. In doing so, we work with and rely on others. This means we have expectations of them. Often, however, these expectations are grounded in our own perspective, rather than in the abilities and motivations of those on our team.

Think about your team for a moment. It's a team composed of people who want to do great work. They want to be part of a great team. And they're very likely doing their absolute best based on what's available to them. Do you believe that? You either do or you don't. In either case, continual improvement is necessary, and therefore personal and team development are necessary.

We can learn a lot about team development from the politician Henry Boyle. He said, "The most important trip you may take in life is meeting people halfway." What we've learned from others, however, is that you need to meet people where they are. For some, that may be halfway. For others, it may be a lot farther than you'd like to travel. But make the trip anyway; if you don't, that person or those people will never live up to your expectations of them.

As a leader, it's certainly right for us to have expectations—high expectations, no doubt. But those expectations shouldn't be based unilaterally on a bias of our personal motivations and abilities; rather, we should determine them through individualized considerations of the abilities of those on our teams.

Individualized consideration is one of the main principles of transformational leadership theory. Whether you're familiar with leadership theories or not, you probably know the value of treating people uniquely—as individuals. Don't work with people from where you are or where you wish they would be. Rather, work with people from where they are. Take the time to know the members of your team. Know their strengths, weaknesses, challenges, and aspirations. Know if they're doing their absolute best based on what's available to them. Then show individualized consideration. Leverage their strengths to enable their success. Doing so will also improve the success of the team and your success as a leader. Work with people from where they are, not where you want them to be.

We explain this rule and concept to leaders when they come to us for guidance, often frustrated from failed attempts at "training" their team. Have you ever had déjà vu moments regarding training sessions, conversations, and what you thought were lessons learned? Maybe it happened during a project or moving a product to market or onboarding a new employee. It's a moment when you think or even say aloud, "How many times do I need to say it?" Or it might be, "How many times do I have to show him?" or "How many times do I have to explain the same thing to her?"

We get it. It can be frustrating. But who's at fault?

We don't always learn things or change our behaviors the first time we're told something, the first time we read something, or the first time we're shown something. In other words, the lessons being taught may not necessarily be learned at the time of the lesson—or even shortly thereafter. In some cases, the lesson may need to be taught or experienced several times before the learning and the associated behavioral change actually occur. This is an important awareness to have: lessons and learning may not be closely associated with time. So aim for immediate learning from all lessons, but don't expect that from any lesson. Manage your frustrations of this reality by realizing that learning is a process and unique to each individual person. Everyone learns at varying rates, and for some, learning will be closely associated with time relative to the lesson; for others, it won't be closely associated with time. It's for this reason that we need to work with people from where they are, not where we'd like them to be.

Rule 35. Don't try to be a friend; rather, be a friendly leader.

Think about your favorite leader. Chances are you consider that person to be friendly—like, the opposite of mean or aloof. Possibly we could substitute the word *friendly* with *kind*. Right?

If effective leadership is about providing intentional influence (and we believe it is), there may be no better way to increase our influence than through kindness. However, that word gets grossly misinterpreted. Colin Powell shared his perspective on this when he said, "Kindness does not mean weakness. Kindness means being empathetic and human. Kindness also means being honest, brutally honest in some cases; this takes managerial and leadership courage. Kindness is not a hard trait. It's about being nice to people. It means offering a smile, a simple note, an authentic gesture of humanness." Your favorite leader was likely kind, because kindness is also about being friendly.

There's a difference between acting friendly and being a friend. Leaders need to lead, rather than trying to be friends. Leadership is not a popularity contest. In fact, if you're trying to please everyone, you're probably not doing your job as a leader! Your effectiveness is not going to be measured by the number of LinkedIn requests you get from direct reports or the number of fives (out of five) you get from your team when they respond to the survey item "I consider my boss a friend."

We should clarify in order to delineate between being friendly and being a friend when in a leadership position. Don't be Facebook friends with your reports, and be careful about getting too close socially. But don't be too distant or aloof either. We know this can seem like a contradiction. What we mean is to give your reports some space. Don't let them feel like they're always involved in work, which can happen if you're on social media or consistently interact socially with people who report to you. Also, it gives you some space from your direct reports.

As the number of members on your team grows, it's impossible to be friends with *all* of them anyway, and you don't want the perception of having favorites. Liane Davey, the psychologist and author, noted a similar sentiment when she wrote, "Investing too much energy in befriending the team confuses the power relationships and ultimately increases the likelihood of a backlash when you begin to exert your control. Most teams are looking for clear, confident leadership. Be friendly and understanding, but don't wait too long to share your vision and to set your standards."

With the differences established, how can one become a friendlier leader? In addition to being an author, Dale Carnegie is also a well-known developer of interpersonal-skills training. He proposed a number of ways that leaders can embody more friendliness. The following is a list of what he included. As you read the list, think about the last time you displayed that act of friendliness, and note what you can do today to show more friendliness:

- Don't criticize, condemn, or complain.
- Give honest, sincere appreciation.
- Arouse in the other person an eager want.
- Become genuinely interested in other people.
- Smile.
- Remember that a person's name is to that person the sweetest and most important sound in any language.
- Be a good listener. Encourage others to talk about themselves.
- Talk in terms of the other person's interests.
- Make the other person feel important—and do it sincerely.

Leadership is about getting results. To do so requires motivated people working in collaboration and coordination with one another. Achieving that requires the power of influence. To maximize your influence, you'll need to recognize that kindness matters—your friendliness matters. Don't spend your time trying to be a friend to your direct reports and larger team; instead, work to be a friendlier leader.

Rule 36. Learn from others and pass it on.

In our lives and careers, effectiveness comes from our ability to continually learn, mainly from those most immediately accessible to us. Sure, we can learn vicariously through books, field guides, and workbooks containing advice—such as this one—but nothing is more effective than getting advice from someone who's immediately accessible to you. These people may be peers, but they can also serve as mentors, advisers, and in some cases, sponsors. For instance, frontline leaders learn most directly from other frontline leaders, individual contributors, and managers. Your mentors and teachers need not be executives. Executives don't always have the time to personally mentor everyone in their organizations, but buddies, peers, and those in your personal network can help you learn throughout your life and career.

On the way up the organizational ladder, you'll learn vicariously through those you don't know and explicitly through those you do know—as well as your own self-reflection on lessons you experience along the way. So find mentors who are teachers, keep being curious and unafraid to ask for help, and continually work to understand the business and its implications on the broader community, how others view it, and your role within it all. We learned this from Louie Ehrlich, a former president of information technology at Chevron, when he recounted his first days at the organization. He said, "It took me about two seconds to realize I don't know anything about the business I am in. If you are new and don't know anything, what are you going to do? You do it through someone else. Meet someone. Form a relationship. Don't be ashamed to go ask. You learn from being curious, unafraid to ask for help."

Jill Saverine, the senior vice president of human resources at Aircastle Limited, explained the importance of having a mentor in terms of that person serving as a "sponsor." This is a person who will take an interest in your career, help you learn and grow, and allow you to make mistakes and learn from them. The most important thing to do is to find a sponsor, mentor, or teacher to do the same for you.

When it's your turn to be a mentor to someone, say yes when asked. That's how you pay for your mentorship: by giving back, paying it forward, and passing it on. You see, leaders don't pay *back* their lessons learned; they pay *forward* those lessons to others who can benefit from their wisdom, experience, perspectives, and insights. We learned from Sara Andrews, a vice president at PepsiCo, about this: "I remember asking my grandma, how can I ever thank the people who helped me in my time of need? How can I pay them back? She said, 'You don't pay them back. You pass it on.'" That's what great mentors and great leaders do—they learn from others who are accessible to them, and they pass it on.

Having a mentor and being a mentor are consistent reminders of the need for the virtues of humility and responsibility—humility to recognize that we don't know everything and that others can teach us, and the responsibility to share our knowledge and experience with those who could benefit from it.

To do it right, mentoring takes time, structure, work, and sometimes, financial resources. But so does almost anything worth considering. Remember rule 7: *know what you're willing to give.* You have to make investments of capital. You can view mentoring and learning as one of the best investments you can make—in others and in yourself. You'll be glad you did.

If you have a mentor, thank that person. If you don't have a mentor, find one. And if you are a mentor, great! If not, think about how and when you will pay it forward.

People Leadership: Reflect, Review, and Commit

- Think of a person on your team or someone you come into contact with on a frequent basis who could use some additional care. What can you do during this next week or month to show this individual that you care? How might you help this person understand his or her value to the team and the larger purpose of his or her work?
- When you think about your life, who's been an exceptional leader who you've had the opportunity to work with? What made the leader exceptional? How much of this leader's success was related to his or her ability to care, connect, and realize the whole person? What can you extract from this person's example and integrate into your leadership style?
- Who on your team *just doesn't get it?* Who's taking longer to comprehend and perform than you'd like? Consider how your expectations might be getting in the way of their development or may not be consistent with their abilities. What would it look like for you to work with these individuals from where they actually are instead of where you hoped they'd be by now? Outline a few specific steps that you could take now to enable better learning and development for them.
- Do you demonstrate kindness in your leadership approach? Are there situations right now where there is confusion regarding being a friend versus acting in a friendly manner? How might you go about clarifying that and creating an approach to leadership where you influence through kindness?

- How can you speed up your personal development by being more intentional about mentoring? Get specific. Who could you learn from by having him or her as a mentor, coach, or teacher? Consider how you might ask that person to help you. Additionally, what lessons could you pass along as a mentor, and who around you could benefit most from those lessons right now?

Team Leadership

Rule 37. Wearing a uniform doesn't make a team.

Who's the best team? We're not asking for your favorite team but rather the *best* team. Maybe you're thinking of a sports team, a team of astronauts, or a medical team operating in an emergency room. Maybe it's a political team, a military unit, your favorite nightly news anchors, or a team of Olympians. Whatever the team you're thinking of right now, its members didn't become great by chance or by wearing the same color scrubs or having the same patches on their uniforms or stickers on their gear. The difference between a group of loosely affiliated people and a high-performing team goes *way* beyond standard apparel or logos.

Any group of people aligned on achieving a purpose has the potential to be great. Any group has the possibility of becoming a high-performing team and realizing greatness. The potential and probability of that actually happening is contingent upon leadership. Realizing greatness is the product of leadership influence.

Among the best teams, there's a leader who has instilled trust, created a compelling direction and vision of the future, established clear roles and expectations, and created a forum or process for active collaboration, feedback, dialogue, action, and follow-through. It's like most everything in life: to achieve greatness, *some assembly is required,* and when it comes to being the best team, it takes significant assembly on the part of the leader, as well as each member of the team.

Think about collaboration, for example. Whatever team you have in mind as being the best is no doubt made up of great collaborators. That doesn't just happen among the members of that team. Great leaders intentionally design for collaboration to occur. Thornton May, the technology futurist and author of *The New Know,* argues that the essence of a team is intentional collaboration. In a recent article, he outlined three important lessons when it comes to establishing effective collaboration among team members. First, leaders must recognize that collaboration can't exist, nor can its value be realized, if there's an absence of desire to collaborate among the members. Second, leaders must understand the collaboration tools available for use and leverage them accordingly. Third, you've got to listen to everyone on the team and throughout the team's network to make collaboration effective. In other words, you've got to have members with a "team" attitude, not a "me" attitude. The best teams are those that are more effective at giving and receiving assistance; they act (individually and collectively) as if everyone has a stake in the outcome.

Think about your team. Is it high performing? Is there room for improvement? If you're aiming for improvement, know that leadership isn't about wielding authority and leveraging positional power. It's about effectively fostering the strengths of a collection of individuals and drawing those individuals into a team in such a way that all their strengths can be expressed, optimized, and leveraged. The best leaders understand that they must give of themselves—relinquishing ego and control, and listening actively and attentively—in order to empower their teams to yield the greatest outcomes. As you assess and hone your own leadership abilities, remember that true leadership is always in service to your team, not in furtherance of your career. Focus on others, and align their strengths to the team's purpose. If you do this effectively, your career will naturally benefit.

Rule 38. Nobody's bigger than the team.

Jack Welch, a former chairman and chief executive officer at General Electric, is famous for getting his teams to deliver results. He viewed managing talent as a paramount function of his role as a leader and often said, "My main job was developing talent." He understood the importance of attracting the best talent and then developing that talent into teams driven by purpose. He compared himself to a gardener: "I was a gardener providing water and other nourishment to our top 750 people." He realized that there are times when some things (and some people) just don't fit with the intentions of the garden. He said, "Of course, I had to pull out some weeds, too." No one can be bigger than the team. The best leaders realize this fact and act based on what's best for the team, not any one member of the team or a subset of the team, because it's about the whole team, not the individual parts.

We've all likely heard that the whole is more than the sum of its parts and that "t-e-a-m" means *together everyone achieves more*. Perhaps one of the greatest speeches about teamwork was delivered in 1983 by Bo Schembechler, the football coach of the University of Michigan Wolverines. In part of the famous speech, he said, "No one is more important than The Team. No coach is more important than The Team. The Team, The Team, The Team, and if we think that way, all of us, everything that you do, you take into consideration what effect does it have on my Team?"

Often within organizations, people lose sight of the real team. People in operations will complain about people in manufacturing, who complain about feature quality from the people in product design, who complain about people in marketing, who complain about salespeople, who complain about people in finance, who complain about everybody. Each perceives the team as his or her unit or division. This is shortsighted and irrational. The team is the whole company, not a subunit of the whole. It's like one of Schembechler's wide receivers saying after a losing game, "Well, I caught all the passes thrown to me by the quarterback. So I'm a winner." No, he's not. If the team didn't win, he's not a winner.

The operation of the whole, not any one player or unit within the whole, is the important part. A team may (and should) be composed of highly talented individuals, but no one is bigger than the team, regardless of how great the person is individually.

Rule 39. Never walk past a mistake.

Like most people, you're probably involved in a lot of interactions throughout any given day. There are meetings to attend, conference calls to join, regular team huddles or stand-ups to hold, and countless conversations to have in hallways, over lunch, and on coffee runs. When's the last time you were participating in one of those interactions and thought, "Wow, this isn't the way we should be going about this work"? Or maybe it went something like, "I'm glad I'm not being held accountable for that decision." When was the last time you came into a conference room that was left a mess from a prior meeting and thought, "Who's going to clean this up?" When was the last time you walked past a few colleagues engaged in a heated debate and thought in a convincing way, "Just keep walking; you've got a meeting to get to, and who knows what they're complaining about this time?" For many people, examples like this are a daily occurrence. We'd bet those same individuals don't find themselves on high-performing teams. These examples are all lost opportunities.

Great leaders and great team members never walk past an opportunity to engage, to fix problems, to right wrongs, or to reinforce a culture of high performance, and that means cleaning the conference room if you find it a mess, straightening a uniform if it's not proper, and correcting behavior if it's not aligned with corporate values. It's worth reiterating rule 22 here: *excellence is not an exception.*

To be sure, we all make mistakes. A mistake here is defined as anything that's wrong, incorrect, out of place, or not as it should be. George Bernard Shaw said, "A life spent making mistakes is not only more honorable, but more useful than a life spent doing nothing." Gandhi said, "Freedom is not worth having if it does not include the freedom to make mistakes." And Albert Einstein is credited with saying, "Anyone who has never made a mistake has never tried anything new." Certainly, we all make mistakes. Not all of us, however, stop to fix mistakes when we see them. That, actually, is perhaps the biggest mistake of all. As such, you can likely already tell that this rule isn't about the virtues or limitation of making mistakes—it's about what we do when we find a mistake.

Leaders address mistakes head on. We're human—mistakes happen all the time. How do you respond when you discover a mistake? The best leaders never walk past a mistake. Doing so is a missed opportunity to learn and to teach. Perhaps even more impactful, walking past a mistake spotlights it as acceptable, something that's tolerated, and over time, this becomes your team's culture. Something wrong doesn't get better with neglect. Mistakes don't turn into learning lessons without some deliberate intervention, reflection, and intention to improve. Be the kind of leader who never walks past a mistake.

Rule 40. Don't confuse being right with getting it right.

If you've ever been part of a high-performing team, you know that the collective group cares less about any one of them being right and much more about making sure they get it right—whatever "it" is. It could be the right solution, the right communication at the right time, or the right market move. Regardless, the end destination, getting it right, is always about a process. It's about the collective inputs from many voices that lead the team of people to optimal solutions. Where you end up might be far from where any one person's original point of view started. That's okay. It's about effective individual contribution in an effort to make sure you get it right over proving that you can be right.

Authors Jim Kouzes and Barry Posner said, "We have to recognize that however smart we are, we're not smarter than everyone else combined." There's great power in collective wisdom, but this is not always obvious to all leaders and all members of a team. John Marcante, the chief information officer at Vanguard, said, "I once thought success meant getting the right answer." We all want to have the right answer. We want to be right all the time. But what John realized is that you're *not* going to be right all the time. Get over thinking that's even a possibility. In today's world and the complexity of our work, we deal more in paradox than in problem-solving. That means our work and the problems we face don't have a single answer; instead, they have multiple alternatives. Great leaders, such as John, recognize this and recognize that the way to address such paradox is through collaboration of thought, sharing multiple perspectives, and focusing effort to identify alternative solutions, rather than an absolute answer.

Any time you focus on being right rather than getting it right, you set up a negative competitive landscape and a zero-sum game. If you're familiar with economics, you know all about zero-sum games—there's always a winner and a loser. If you're on a team in which members feel some will win and some will lose, you *all* lose every time. A better approach is a team win: the team members either win together, or they lose together. This approach fosters a culture in which people encourage one another, cheer for one another, and enable one another's success because the win of a teammate is a win for the team—a win for everyone.

Rule 41. Find a way to say yes.

Cheryl Smith was a chief information officer for a large organization. In a recent conversation with her, we learned an important rule about team leadership. To truly build a team that has ownership, commitment, and engagement, "say yes as often as possible."

High-performing teams are often composed of smart people who work hard. Cheryl knows this and was asked once by a team of IT professionals, "Can we have a game room?" Now, for context, this company wasn't a start-up, nor was it one that had fully stocked refrigerators of Red Bull or "grown-up" slides that span three stories of the building for use rather than taking the elevator or stairs. But she knew that saying yes would be a win for the IT group and the company. The people on her team worked hard on complex projects, and Cheryl was interested in making sure they didn't suffer burnout from fatigue. She was interested in the whole (twenty-four-hour) person, not just the (eight-hour) employee. She knew that saying yes would be a motivator. And in the case of a game room and a number of other requests that you likely get on a regular basis, saying no would be easy, and in some of those cases, rational and prudent. Cheryl said yes and figured out a way to make it work, not just for her IT team but for the whole company.

Shortly after the lesson learned from Cheryl, we read an article by Kathryn Schulz in *The New Yorker* in which she said that saying yes is the first rule of improv. As it turns out, saying yes is not just a motivator for a period of time but also a way to maintain energy, imagination, and collaboration. She goes on to say, "While sometimes impractical, dangerous, or just plain dumb, saying yes to as much stuff as possible is, overall, a pretty good strategy for getting through life." Many times, an unbridled yes may not be the optimal response. In these cases, we're fans of the "yes, and here's how" response, clarifying the conditions on which the yes is based.

Akin to the power of "yes," there's power of "both-and." Even when you say yes often, there will be times when disagreements erupt. As great as it is to have a big-screen television, a foosball table, a couple of recliners, a dartboard, and a general lounge area in a game room for employees to destress and reenergize, there will be some who disapprove. You'll be questioned, "Why is the game room on the fourth floor and not the fifth floor?" and "Why foosball and not ping-pong?" You can likely imagine other questions, too. The best leaders try to negotiate for both-and solutions, not either-or. But it's not likely to be easy, yet it's always likely to be valuable.

As we close out this rule, keep in mind that while it's easy to say no, it's also easy to take sides. It takes more effort, time, and commitment to uncover the both-and solution in disagreements, but as with the power of yes, the best leaders know that a both-and strategy is pretty good for getting through life and career. The people asking will be grateful, and you'll most likely find yourself with a more engaged group of individuals.

Rule 42. When it comes to engagement, you won't get everyone.

Research has shown that the lack of employee engagement—or disengagement—costs companies over $550 billion in lost productivity every year. No wonder engagement is such a hot topic these days! Think about your own organization. What's the engagement rate?

If your organization is like most, Gallup studies say it'll be around one-third. On average, only one-third of the employees in your organization are fully engaged. What would happen if you were able to move that percentage higher? Forget about getting to 100 percent. You're not going to get there. As Tom Murphy, the chief information officer at University of Pennsylvania, reminded us, "You're not going to get everyone. While that shouldn't stop you from trying, you're just not going to get 100 percent engagement. But you don't need 100 percent to be effective and move the organization forward." You don't need 100 percent engagement, consensus, or buy-in before making a decision, and you don't need the same percentage to be an effective leader, team, or company.

As Aon Hewitt's *Trends in Global Employee Engagement* studies have shown, if you can increase engagement by 5 percent, your revenues will increase 3 percent the subsequent year. The Workplace Research Foundation's studies have seen profits per employee go up more than $2,000 if employee engagement increases by 10 percent. In short, if you move the dial just a bit when it comes to engagement, the results are significant. Kevin Kruse, the best-selling author and regular contributor to the *New York Times*, explained it in a cause-effect way: "Engaged employees lead to higher service, quality, and productivity, which leads to higher customer satisfaction, which leads to increased sales (repeat business and referrals), which leads to higher levels of profit, which leads to higher shareholder returns." It's significant.

So how do the best leaders increase engagement? Let's get the best advice again from Tom Murphy: "Engagement occurs locally. Any leader can give a great speech to rally the troops, but that won't help engagement. Engagement is fostered and anchored closest to the employee. Her or his immediate supervisor and teammates will be the influential forces. So, make sure they are equipped to drive engagement."

Also, as a reminder, when it comes to those employees closest to you, make sure you're considering the whole person. Anne M. Mulcahy, a former chairman and chief executive officer at Xerox Corporation, astutely noted, "Employees who believe that management is concerned about them as a whole person—not just an employee—are more productive, more satisfied, more fulfilled." Satisfied employees are much more engaged than those who are dissatisfied, and quite frankly, they're happier. As Michal Addady's study in *Fortune* magazine noted, "Being happy at work really makes you more productive."

While you may not get everyone fully engaged, don't let that reality impede your progress. It's always possible to increase engagement just slightly, and the results are worth your effort.

Rule 43. You're not your team, but you're defined by your team.

One of our favorite cities to visit is Denver, Colorado. If you've been there, you probably have a good idea of why. If you haven't been, you should visit sometime. Denver, the Mile-High City, is known for many things: being beautifully decorated by the Rocky Mountains, having more than three hundred days of sunshine each year, having some of the best parks in the world, and being the location of one of our favorite places to eat, the Denver Chophouse. Interestingly, each of these things Denver is known for isn't actually the city itself. The city (any city, for that matter) is defined by the amenities and sights within it and the experiences afforded because of them.

Let's go back to that restaurant for an example. The Denver Chophouse is a can't-miss eatery for anyone who likes big plates of perfectly cooked meals. In addition to the fantastic food, the Chophouse also boasts an almost perfect atmosphere, wonderful menu variety, and simply fantastic service. None of these alone are the restaurant. However, the restaurant is defined by the culmination of all of these features. In fact, if you went online to Yelp, TripAdvisor, or any other rating website, you'd see each of these aspects showing up as descriptors. People can't describe the restaurant outside of the features that define it. There's no way to describe the restaurant without defining what makes the experience so enjoyable.

The last time we were at the Denver Chophouse, we saw one of the chefs on his way out of the restaurant. We wondered whether it was the same person who had cooked the delicious meal we'd just savored. With the image of a chef fresh in our minds and the taste of our salad, potato, and steak still in our mouths, we couldn't help but think that a chef is almost entirely defined by the quality of the food that he or she produces. (Most chefs are never actually seen!) And the food created is defined by the quality of the ingredients and the mixtures and proportions that are represented. The same could be said of so many things, not the least of which is leadership. That brings us to this rule: *you're not your team, but you're defined by your team.*

In the same way that a chef is not a restaurant, you're not your team. The quality of the chef will be defined by the quality of the food produced. Equally, when it comes to effectiveness (like your personal brand), it's not defined by you, but rather your team and others beyond the team.

Let's think about that a bit more. Your team's accomplishments, activities, and behaviors have your fingerprints on them for others to see. In short, when others see your team and the work produced by and through that team, they see you. They see your leadership, your character, and your competency. Leaders harness time, energy, enthusiasm, intellect, collaboration, and ability from each team member.

Through the art of their leadership, truly exceptional leaders enable the team to accomplish more than the science of management says would otherwise be possible. As a team, they're able to create more than what any one of them alone, or a subset of them, could have. The leader isn't the team but an individual member on the team, and because of that, the best leaders—just like the best teams—measure their effectiveness in terms of collective achievement, not individual advancement. Your success is not yours alone. Your leadership and your successes will be defined by the performance of your team.

Rule 44. Your success is a social journey.

One truism about individual success is that it's never individual success. Your success isn't yours alone. Success is a social journey.

Now, to be sure, any success requires some individual contribution—perhaps a lot of it. However, any individual who has ever accomplished something was at one time given a chance to succeed. That chance was provided (and perhaps encouraged) by another person. When individual success is diagnosed, we often find teams of people around that individual who've helped make that success possible. Even a sumo wrestler, solo musician, highest-ranking executive, or others who are seemingly responsible for their own success have had mentors, coaches, supporters, and teams. There's no journey, especially a successful leadership journey, that's traveled alone. It's a social journey.

Keep this in mind as you go about your work and life. You need people around you. You need collaborators. You need people with similar and differing perspectives. You need your team. You need to foster "teamness" or teamwork. Your success depends on it. Your success will be based on your ability to engage others on a social journey, and your effectiveness is grounded in positive collaboration among those on the journey together.

Life, and the work throughout it, can be a real joy—and it should be. Certainly, it'll be full of ups and downs, transformational breakthroughs, varying degrees of setbacks, fear, fast progress, slow change, distractions, absolute focus, trade-offs, and a few big bets that hopefully prove to be worth it. One common variable through it all is people. You never go it alone. You never journey alone. And you certainly never succeed alone. It's the people on your team, working in collaboration, who make all the difference in who you are and the success you realize.

Team Leadership: Reflect, Review, and Commit

- Think about what you can do to better "assemble" your team for maximum performance. Document a specific activity that you can engage in during the next week or month to build a greater sense of unity and cohesion among your team. It doesn't need to be elaborate, expensive, or time consuming.

- In being honest with yourself, is there a current mistake that you've ignored or are currently ignoring that needs your attention? How might things look different if you addressed this? What do you need to do to give your attention to this matter right now?

- Where's a spirit of competition getting in the way of greater success? Do you or someone on your team struggle with the desire to be right more than getting it right? What structures can you put into place as a leader that'll intensify the goal of getting it right versus the personal need to be right?

- Is there something or someone that you recently said "no" to that could possibly have been answered with a "yes" or a "yes, and here's how" response? What can you learn from this situation that you can take with you for the next time?

- What experiences are you creating for your team? While you go about your work of getting things done, what's the experience like for the members? Outside of project outcomes, what can you do to enhance the experience that'll create a positive impact long beyond the project end date?

Self-Leadership

Rule 45. Life's not fair; get used to it.

Many life lessons are simple truisms that we learned as children and carry with us throughout our adult lives. One of the earliest and truest life lessons has to be "life's not fair." How many times did you hear that growing up? It was likely early in life that you realized just how true that short statement is. The fact that life's not fair was certainly evident by the time you were three or four years of age (or maybe a lot earlier, if you have siblings).

Bill Gates, the founder of Microsoft and philanthropist, once gave a speech in which he talked about "rules your kids did not and will not learn in school." Guess what the number one rule on that list was? Yep, you got it! "Life is not fair—get used to it." It's great advice, and although it's been taught to us from an early age, we may still struggle with this lesson from time to time.

When we're born, we all fall somewhere along the "fairness continuum." Some are born into fortune, some into immediate fame, others into opposite and extreme conditions, and still others somewhere between the extremes. We have no choice about the demographics or socioeconomic situations that we're born into. Although we may have limited choice at birth and during the immediate years that follow, as we get older, our choices increase.

In particular, how we choose to view the fairness or unfairness of life changes.

A great number of people have squandered the advantages they were born into. And a great number of people have overcome the extreme conditions they were born into. We learn, sooner or later, that life and its fairness are a state of mind. The most productive people and all great leaders know this. They don't dwell on the fact that life's not fair or feel victimized because of it. Rather, they realize that any effort to complain and blame does little to address the underlying issue, which is how to overcome the reality of fairness to realize greatness.

Any effort to simply complain and blame is the path of least resistance and is what a lot of people choose, unfortunately. Choosing to dwell on an unfair situation comes at a major opportunity cost of your effort, time, and capability. It's your choice to decide what to do with the world as you find it. We all know from experience that we'll find the world unfair from time to time or maybe even quite often. What will you do? What do you do today? What have you done in the past?

A senior vice president at a supply-chain logistics company told us, "Life is really all about what happens to you and how you then react. What happens to you is about ten percent of life. Ninety percent is how you then react to it. That is what you have control of and how you react is based upon your past experience and those experiences—good, bad, indifferent—are what makes your ninety percent stronger moving forward." What we are referring to here is resilience—the ability of a leader to recover from difficulties and setbacks. All leaders experience setbacks; it just comes with the job. The best leaders realize setbacks will occur because life's not fair, but they are not willing to accept failure because of them. They absorb the impacts, reflect on what went wrong, adjust as needed, and once again take action to gain forward momentum.

What will you do with the world as you find it? It won't always be fair. You'll be faced with difficult changes in your industry. You'll inherit weak teams. You'll experience less-than-good bosses. You'll be forced to participate in company politics. You'll put in incredible amounts of work that'll go unnoticed and might even get falsely credited to other individuals. There may also be the occasion that "fairness" will be weighted in your favor.

What will you do? Will you allow it to paralyze you and limit you to simply follow the path of least resistance? Or will you change your mind about fairness and tackle the issues head on? It's true that life's not fair. It's also true that you choose your path. How will you choose?

Rule 46. You can't control your situation, but you can control your choice.

Many people are familiar with the name Victor Frankl. He's a hero. He's a Holocaust survivor and author of *Man's Search for Meaning*, in which he chronicled his experiences as an inmate at the Auschwitz concentration camp. Frankl, a neurologist and psychiatrist, knew all about the fairness of life. He also knew the importance of mind-set, which was magnified while imprisoned. His general hypothesis was that the way a prisoner imagined the future, either positively or negatively, affected his or her longevity. While in the concentration camp, Frankl realized that "everything can be taken from a man but one thing; the last of the human freedoms—to choose one's attitude in any given set of circumstances, to choose one's own way."

The challenges we face can never be compared to those of Victor Frankl or the millions of others who suffered in concentration camps. But we all can learn from Frankl's perspective and experiences about choice. We may not always find the world to our liking. Indeed, we may find the world a dark place at times. The questions we'll be faced with are what we will do and how it will affect our mindset.

In *Man's Search for Meaning*, Frankl wrote, "Man's main concern is not to gain pleasure or to avoid pain, but rather to see a meaning in his life." What are you imagining as your future? What are you imagining as your meaning in life? How's that vision affecting your longevity in your current situation, as well as those around you—those you lead?

You cannot control every situation you encounter. You can, however, control your imagined future and your choices. Your imagined future—that which is possible every day and every moment of every day—will affect your longevity. And the choices you make will precede the actions you take. The best leaders spend their time on what they can do, rather than dwelling on any limiting factors, conditions, or abilities that highlight what they can't do. We were reminded of this by Cynthia Trudell, the chief human resources officer at PepsiCo, who said, "You are who you are. Be that and figure out how that is important to others."

You can't be who you aren't. It's for this reason Oscar Wilde said, "Be yourself. Everyone else is taken." We learned a similar lesson from Linda Betz, the chief information security officer at Travelers Companies, who said, "I play my game. I focus on what I am good at." To be most successful, you've got to leverage your strengths.

If you're like most people, you have created lists of your strengths and weaknesses a time or two (or twelve) at varying points throughout your life and career. For a long time, consultants, coaches, and psychologists recommended placing focus on improving weaknesses. However, the most successful among us do just the opposite: they focus on their strengths to the point of trying to make them even stronger. The best professional running backs in the National Football League don't practice tackling to be better as linebackers or throwing in an effort to become better quarterbacks. The best pitchers in Major League Baseball don't take extra batting practice. The best leaders do the same; they don't focus on who they're not and what they can't do. Those who are the best (the very best) focus on their core strengths and work to exploit those strengths for their own gain and in support of their team to accomplish shared goals.

Situations will continue to change. That's something you cannot control. When faced with challenges, choose your own way by focusing on a positive mindset and leveraging your strengths to reach your envisioned future state.

Rule 47. You bring your weather.

Recently, each of the authors had an opportunity to take a vacation. The destinations of choice were Arizona, Florida, and Hawaii. You can immediately recognize these as desired destinations for many people looking to escape the coldness and cloudiness of other places in the world. Certainly, there are many other places in the world people escape to when looking to get away. These locations normally share one common element: weather. Simply put, weather affects comfort. Weather influences moods and the way people feel.

The word *climate* is often used to classify different weather conditions. That same word, *climate,* is also used to describe workplace conditions. In other words, how does the office feel? Is there a positive climate or a negative climate?

Just like weather systems and geographical locations, you, too, bring weather with you when and where you show up in the world. That positive or negative climate in the workplace isn't just happenstance. It exists because people make it happen. It's a by-product of the people who are part of that system. Leaders bring the weather. Everyone brings weather. What kind of weather do you bring? Said another way, what shows up when you do?

This is a self-check question—and an important one. Think about your day, the meetings you attend, the people you meet, and the work you do. Think about how you show up. Do you have a smile on your face or a frown? Are you a solutions collaborator or the person who always raises issues? Are you a problem solver or passive-aggressive? Are you "we" focused or "me" focused? Do you share and facilitate collaboration or roll your eyes in disgust?

How you show up matters because it's a representation of your attitude. More importantly, when you're a leader, people are always watching you. You're always influencing, while others are always judging. Whether you want to or not, you're affecting those around you.

We've all likely heard the sentiment that we can't create every situation, but we can choose how to act in every situation. Tracey Arnish, the chief talent officer at SAP, has said, "Life is about perspective. The only thing you can control is how you choose to show up." Indeed, and how you do that affects everyone in your path.

Next time you walk through the doors of your company or into a meeting room, ask yourself what's showing up. Ask, "What kind of weather am I bringing?" Your attitude, conviction, and demeanor can be the difference between success or failure. And it will influence everyone around you. So always consider the impact of your weather and the climate you create.

Rule 48. You can't wait to be great.

How often have you been disengaged because you saw others disengaged? How often have you said or thought that you're not going to give 100 percent of your skills and abilities because you think your boss is an idiot, your team is just not worth it, or you're not getting paid enough or don't have the right title, or it's just not worth your time? This is understandable sometimes, but it's also illogical.

We understand it because you want to feel and see a sense of fairness. But we all know from rule 45 that *life's not fair*. What you should be aware of is the fact that you're always being watched. Whether you want to be or not, you are. And more than just being watched, you're being judged.

You're being watched all the time, and people are making judgments about you all the time. If you don't feel that you have a great leader or boss or manager and therefore are not going to show up in a great way, how then do you show up? If it's not your best, then it's something closer to average or worse, and that's how people see you. So the fact that you're waiting for someone around you to be great (or greater) is causing you to not be great. How illogical is that?

You don't have control over who your boss is. You don't always have control over who's on your team. You do, however, have control over how you show up. If you show up in average ways, you're going to find averageness all around you. If you think there's averageness all around you and you show up in the great way you're capable of, you'll start to see the average get better. People aren't watching you only to make judgments; more likely, they're watching you to take cues as to how to make sense of a very complex world and, in turn, how to act themselves. When they see mediocrity, they'll base their expectations around that level of performance and come to believe that averageness is okay, desired, or maybe even the best that's possible.

Ryan Russell, who leads the human-centered design work at Amazon, reminded us that there's a big difference in knowing the difference between average and great. He said, "When you have great people, you attract great people. Great people make people feel great." That, in part, is what the best leaders do. And it's what the best followers do, too. Through our actions, we help enable people to do great things and in that process, we attract great people, and they also attract great people. If we have an average manager, we can help that person get better. If we have an average teammate, we can help that person get better. But we can help them get better only if we choose to be great all the time. Remember rule 22: *excellence is not an exception.*

You can't wait to have a great leader or great teammates for you to show up in a great way. Make the conscious decision to show up great and to be great all the time.

Now you might think that "all the time" is a lot. Yes, it is. We've learned from great leaders that the best never give up their enthusiasm to be great and to do great things. They make the decision to be great every day. You probably recall Louie Ehrlich's comment about always influencing those around you. The former president of IT and chief information officer at Chevron said, "Everything you do has an influence, whether you like it or not." There's no escaping that fact as a leader. You're always being watched, and your actions are always influencing others.

Rule 49. You're leading and leaving a legacy; act accordingly.

Your actions and reactions have influence. Whether you're intentional about how you show up or not, your presence will define you. You're either building up or tearing down your personal brand, team culture, and those around you with every action every day. That might be hard to think about—every action, every day? Yes, every action, every day! Although the last rule talked about this, it's important enough to reiterate it in its own rule.

David Whyte is a poet, speaker, and the author of *The Heart Aroused: Poetry and the Preservation of the Soul in Corporate America.* He found that "every action taken, from the moment we switch off the alarm clock in the morning to the way we write a line of poetry or design a product, has the potential to change the world, leave it cold with indifference, or perhaps more commonly, nudge it infinitesimally in the direction of good or evil." Similarly, Jody Davids, a senior vice president at PepsiCo and author of *A Tale of Two Heroes*, said that you must "know that you will have a legacy. Act accordingly."

Everything we do is creating influence and our legacy. Our action or inaction, our speech or silence, our engagement or disengagement—everything we do, intentionally or unintentionally, is being observed by others and will determine our legacy. Act accordingly indeed!

Now the fact that everything you do creates influence can lead to paranoia. That's certainly not our intent. It's simply meant to provide an awareness of how you choose to show up. Any action without this rule (and others) in mind may very well result in influencing others in a way that's not aligned with the kind of leader we want to be. Tom Murphy, the chief information officer at the University of Pennsylvania, shared a lesson he learned about his actions getting in the way of his message. He had just given a motivational talk to his staff. He left them energized and inspired about organizational changes on the horizon. As he left a meeting later that day, he walked across the sky-bridge spanning two buildings of the company. It was there that someone else noticed him portraying a negative demeanor. His head was down, his shoulders were slouched, and his gaze was a distant stare. He said, "I had no idea I was conveying that message until it was pointed out to me. That was certainly not my intention, but I learned quickly that I can completely undo everything I just said by the nonverbal signals I send. As leaders, we need to be self-aware. We need to realize that we're on stage all the time and people are watching and taking cues from not only the verbal, but also the nonverbal messages we send. We're always being judged and always influencing those around us."

Think about your role in your organization, in your family, and in your community. Think about the activities and experiences you face every day. Some, no doubt, are joyous. Others may challenge your beliefs. It's for this reason that Marc Varner, the chief information security officer at YUM! Brands, told us, "Bad days will come that will put you under pressure and you may not act the way you would want to act. It's because those days will come that you need to know who you are, what you stand for, and what you want to be known for." Your actions in these situations will be your legacy.

We all face moments when the makeup of our legacy is threatened to be lost and when "positive" leadership seems out of reach, yet it's times like these that require us to demonstrate our positivity, hope, and leadership. It's during times like these that we need to leverage care, consideration, and patience. It's during times like these that we need to know who we are, the brand we aim to display, what we stand for, and the legacy we want to leave. It's times like these that make us need to know what we'll do with the world as we find it. It's times like these that you must know the answer to the question, what shows up when I do?

This question is about presence and intentionality. The best leaders never forget that whether you're intentional or not, your presence shows up. So be more than simply prepared for bad days and challenging circumstances. Be intentional!

Be intentional about who you are and what you do. Be intentional about your attitude, thoughts, actions and reactions, mental readiness, emotional balance, and physical presence. Be intentional about it all. Your legacy is depending upon it and will be defined by it.

Self-Leadership: Reflect, Review, and Commit

- Think of a situation you've encountered recently that wasn't fair. Seriously, it just shouldn't have been that way. Instead of dwelling on it and spending precious energy, what's your next best move to work with the situation as it is?

- If you were to candidly describe the impact you make and the climate you create when you show up, what does it look like? Describe it as weather. Is it an attractive weather pattern, or is it cold and uncomfortable? Record several concrete ways that you can positively affect the climate when you show up.

- What's an area in your life or in your work where you've succumbed to averageness—to mediocrity—because you're waiting on something or someone to change before giving your best? What's standing in the way of you being great? Consider a few ways you can improve your mindset and take initial action toward maximum engagement and contribution. If you were to show up with maximum engagement, what would that mean for that situation and the people involved?

- Think about a specific role you have in your organization, family, or community. As you consider the impression you're making and the legacy you're leaving, what's something you could be more intentional about, something that could create a more positive impression? Can you start that this week?

Section 3: Station Break

When it comes to leadership, it's all about aligning the effort of people, knocking down barriers for them, overcoming challenges, and collaborating to accomplish something you couldn't have done alone. It's all about people. And how you work with people creates the culture and climate you work in. The best leaders know that getting the best out of people requires positive communication in an effort to establish positive meaning in the work being performed and to create positive relationships with and among people. The better you can align people's work while having genuine individualized consideration for each person, the better your results will be as a leader and a team.

Speaking of a team, your Amtrak team has moved you eastward on your journey from Seattle to Chicago. By this time, you're likely at the Wisconsin Dells station stop. Or maybe you've made it to Portage, Wisconsin. The meaning of portage is literally the carrying of a boat or its cargo between two navigable waters. The two navigable waters there are the Fox River and the Wisconsin River. To be successful at portaging a boat or its cargo, you're going to need people, which makes this a good place to think about people leadership, team leadership, and self-leadership.

Pause, reflect, and talk with your friends, neighbors, colleagues, and other leaders about where you are and where you're going. As you do so, remember the prior rules. The first section covered fourteen rules regarding the foundation of leadership—mindset, purpose, and perspective. Section 2 covered seventeen rules on vision, preparation, and action that serve as the pillars of effective leadership. Section 3 detailed rules about how leaders lead people (the framework that connects the leadership pillars). The focus was all about people leadership, team leadership, and self-leadership.

Spend some time here to think about the eighteen rules from this section and the prior thirty-one rules from the other sections. While you think about these rules, consider the following.

- Which rules really resonated with you pertaining to this section? How do you intend to put them into practice in the near future?
- What aspects of leading people are important to you, and what rule or rules might you add to this section?

Your success as a leader requires the strength and efficacy of a strong foundation (your mindset, purpose, and perspective) as well as the pillars of leadership (your vision, preparation, and action). But, importantly, it also requires engagement with people, and that's been the focus of this station break.

Section 4
The Learning Practices of Great Leaders and Leadership

Leadership isn't a capability born into a select few but a learnable set of behaviors available to everyone. However, great leadership doesn't happen by accident. It happens by learning. According to Brian Herbert, a *New York Times* best-selling author, "The capacity to learn is a gift; the ability to learn is a skill; the willingness to learn is a choice." It's a fact: learning is a choice, and the more disciplined your approach to learning leadership, the better your capability to lead becomes. In short, great leaders are great learners of leadership.

A leader's effectiveness is enabled because of his or her discipline to continually learn. As you've learned from the rules in this workbook, the foundation of leadership is the core of any leader's capability (section 1). The three pillars of leadership that rise up from that foundation strengthen it and further enable the leader's capability (section 2). The interactions leaders have with their teams drive attitude and performance (section 3). What you'll learn from the five rules on *learning* in section 4 is that it's the only way a leader can sustain effectiveness over time.

Learning

Rule 50.	Leadership's a moving target.
Rule 51.	Feedback accelerates learning, which accelerates greatness.
Rule 52.	If you're not learning, you're in trouble.
Rule 53.	There will be good days and bad days; learn from both.
Rule 54.	Look for your next best move.

Because of the ever-changing situations, variables, conditions, and scenarios that leaders face, there's no silver bullet, no one way, and no one-size-fits-all approach or absolute formula for successful leadership. The most effective leaders adapt their leadership based on situations, variables, conditions, and scenarios, which makes learning continually necessary.

Like leadership, learning is fundamentally adaptive and is important relative to the first rule in this section: *leadership is a moving target.* It's easy for most people to understand the premise of a moving target. Our markets change. Our landscapes change. Our environments change. Our lives change. Everything around us is moving, and we must adapt as well. That's easy to understand. What's much more difficult to understand, and do, is to actually change—to change perspective, to change our approach, to change our mind, or to change our behavior. However, if we're aiming for sustained success, we must change, and to do so, we must learn.

The best leaders know that a previously made successful decision may not yield success again if anything or anyone around them has changed, which is likely the case. The difference between a leader having a single success and leaders with multiple successes is their ability to move quickly, learn quickly, and adapt quickly. Just as it's important for organizations and teams within them to continually improve, it's important for leaders to do the same.

We noted in section 2 that if you're going to become the leader you aspire to be, you're going to have to work at it. That means you're going to have to change. But to know *what* to change, you're going to have to learn.

It's true that if you're not learning, you're in trouble. There's simply too much complexity in our work and too much change in life to think that you know it all or even know *enough* at any given point in time. In fact, just at the point when you think you may know something, it's already becoming obsolete. There's a shelf life or expiration date to what we know and how we go about our work.

The speed of technology, innovation, media, discovery, exploration, and development are all converging to compress the shelf life of what we know, how we know it, and how we do things. It's proving the fact that today's knowledge won't be sufficient for the challenges we face tomorrow. There are things we don't know today that we'll need to know in the future to be effective. So we've got to learn. We've got to learn when things go well. We've got to learn when things go poorly. We've got to learn all the time and get comfortable with not knowing as part of a learning process—as part of a leadership process.

Not knowing can be frustrating. The best leaders know that there's always more to know and that the most important effort in life and career is to reflect, reset, and improve. It's from this process that great leaders continue to get better and prepare themselves for their next challenge.

As you study the five rules in this section, consider the prior rules. You'll no doubt see a direct connection back to section 1. Indeed, there's a continuing loop of these rules—from the leadership rules in section 4 to the mindset, purpose, and perspective rules in section 1. It's the Möbius strip of leadership, a continuation without a beginning or end.

If you've studied mathematics, you likely have experience with the Möbius strip (illustrated here) or what mathematicians may refer to as orientability. That's a fancy word for a property of surfaces that measure the possibility of making a consistent choice of surface normal at every point on the surface. Since that can be confusing, perhaps a simpler explanation is that there's no start or end, no up or down, no left or right, no outer edge or inner edge. It's continual, like the process of leadership. It's an ongoing process.

As you work to improve from learning, you'll find yourself determining what's possible. As you know, that's a mindset. So as you determine what's possible and what's next, pause and reflect. See yourself through the behaviors you've exhibited with others rather than the milestones you've achieved. Your interactions with others, not the end goals you've accomplished, define your leadership. Reflect on those behaviors. Isolate the improvements, adapt, and prepare yourself to move on to what's next. Mark the rules you want to adopt as your own and share your new lessons and key takeaways with others. Document the rules that, when put into practice, will make you an even better leader.

Learning

Rule 50. Leadership's a moving target.

How many times have you seen or heard of a great leader leaving one team or organization to go to another one and not being able to duplicate his or her earlier success? This happens quite often. There's no scientific formula for great leadership, and the constancy of change in the variables being managed—personnel, products, processes, financing, competition, customer demand, sense of urgency, expectations—will prevent any single formula from ever becoming a proof. Those who have been successful have been so because they took the time necessary to understand the strengths in the resources they have, aligned those strengths to a vision, set absolute expectations for each member of their teams, and had a disciplined bias toward action, follow-up, follow-through, and continual improvement until the vision was realized. This is not a formula for the simple fact that the outcome is not guaranteed.

Part of continual improvement involves trading out variables and making changes based on how close—or far away—you're getting to your targeted future state. The best leaders know that today's knowledge and skill won't be sufficient to address the challenges of tomorrow. Change is always needed because the target is always moving, and therefore learning is always essential.

Several years ago, Jeff Immelt, a former chairman and chief executive officer at General Electric, gave a lecture at Stanford University. During his lecture, he directed a point to the students, but it was important for the faculty and administrators gathered there to hear it as well. His point was about the fleeting shelf life of knowledge. He said, "The things you're learning, while you're here [in college] are going to be pretty irrelevant relatively soon." He's not the only one noticing the need for continual learning. His predecessor, Jack Welch, famously said, "An organization's ability to learn, and translate that learning into action rapidly, is the greatest competitive advantage." Samuel Arbesman, a senior scholar at the Kauffman Foundation and a research fellow at the Institute for Quantitative Social Science at Harvard University, wrote about this phenomenon in his book *The Half-Life of Facts: Why Everything Has an Expiration Date*. Thirty years prior to that book, Buckminster Fuller, the systems theorist, architect, and author, detailed the Knowledge Doubling Curve in his book *The Critical Path*.

The Knowledge Doubling Curve, as its name may imply, is an estimate of how much time it takes for knowledge to double. At the turn of the twentieth century, the Knowledge Doubling Curve was estimated to be one hundred years. The Internet and Internet of Things have changed the pace of knowledge drastically, to the point that many estimate the curve to currently be about twelve years but anticipate it being twelve hours (yes, you read that right—*twelve hours*) very soon. Incredible, huh? This means that current knowledge is becoming outdated more quickly, and the pace at which people must learn has to speed up. Within this understanding is the awareness that we just won't know everything at any given point in time because the variables around us and our knowledge (of anything) are moving targets with an increasingly limited shelf life. The best we can do is learn—and fast.

It's true. The innovations of tomorrow and solutions to our problems tomorrow won't be based on what we know today. As well, the leadership techniques that work today likely won't be as effective in the future. The moving target of leadership requires leaders to move as well. Understanding where to move, and how, is found in learning.

Rule 51. Feedback accelerates learning, which accelerates greatness.

Do you remember the days before the existence and use of any Global Positioning System (GPS)? It's a wonder we ever got where we were going! In order to reasonably get to somewhere new, you had to download and print directions from the Internet, buy a map from a gas station attendant, or stop by your local AAA office to get detailed route directions from where you currently were to where you were aiming to be. Those resources worked really well if you stayed on course and knew where you were at all times relative to the map.

An executive in our research shared this story: "We once were on a trip to the Boundary Waters in upper Minnesota and lower Canada. What a beautiful and vast place! Over ten days, we journeyed 120 miles by canoe and foot. We crossed over twenty lakes. We had many maps with us on that journey. Those maps were a lifesaver. The critical nature of navigating that terrain hinged on our ability to always know where we were on the map."

You see, maps are virtually useless if you don't know where you are. The power of modern GPS is location and continual feedback. The satellites used for GPS tracking consistently provide you feedback relative to where you currently are in position to where you want to be. They've changed our navigational lives, and location and feedback will change your professional and personal life in much the same way. If you're looking to get somewhere new, there's no way better than from feedback relative to where you currently are and where you want to be.

Feedback is a gift. It's an accelerator to realizing your vision, achieving greatness, and assuring continual improvement. Cheryl Smith realized the power and importance of feedback while navigating to the role of chief information officer at McKesson. She reminded us that in any (and every) interaction with your supervising manager, peers, customers, and subordinates, it's valuable to get feedback. Ask these questions: "What am I doing that you want me to continue doing? What am I doing that you want me to stop doing or change? And, what am I not doing that you want me to start doing?" These questions help to maintain alignment with expectations and build a rapport that makes it easier to point out issues when they do arise—and they *will* arise, whether you're in the Boundary Waters or any organization.

In addition to asking the questions Cheryl outlined of your boss and others, you can use them to test your leadership among your team. Turn them into statements, and even add to them a bit to help make sure you're accelerating greatness for others by helping them learn through feedback. Answering yes or no to the following every week, if not every day, can help your team get better individually and collectively:

- I gave constructive feedback today that will help my team increase performance.
- I showed genuine care, concern, and individualized consideration today.
- I helped align priorities and expectations to our vision today.
- I shared information from my meetings with my team to help them see the larger picture of the enterprise and meaning in their work.
- I helped my team members with their individual development plans and career projection.

Just as you should always be making an effort to both be and have a mentor, you should also work hard to both solicit and provide feedback—continually! Be serious about feedback, because feedback accelerates learning, which accelerates greatness.

Rule 52. If you're not learning, you're in trouble.

Those who can learn the fastest can effect and adopt change the fastest. This doesn't mean it's easy to do, but it certainly is easy to understand how learning can create a differentiating factor among teams and organizations. Think about Google or Amazon or Apple or any other industry-leading organization. They're in those positions because of their ability to see market needs, change current models, and deliver quality and excellence being demanded in products and services. They're unique. We all know the importance learning plays in creating this uniqueness.

It's true that if you're not learning, you're in trouble. We had the good fortune recently to meet with Marshall Goldsmith, during which time he explained the connection between learning and leadership. We had asked, "What is a defining characteristic of a great leader?" That's a pretty standard question for an executive coach, but his response is what stuck with us and is the pertinent part of the story for this rule. Without hesitation he said, "All of the great leaders I have coached have the following in common—they're learners." In anything they do every day, from market meetings to product briefings to everything, they want to learn about what's going on around them and how effective they're being through their leadership. Regardless of your situation, context, project, role—anything—"go in as a learner." That's what the best leaders do.

Marshall's point is a good reminder for us, because sometimes we can forget about learning. We don't forget about its importance, but we forget to make it happen. Here's why—most of us, probably all of us, have had success in life and career. As we instructed in rule 13, *stop believing everything you think*—our success can hold us back due to blind spots or even delusion. Marshall would say that this delusion can occur because successful people have four key beliefs: "I have succeeded, I can succeed, I will succeed, and I choose to succeed." These beliefs are all quite positive. They're optimistic. Each belief can serve as a force multiplier to effect more success, growth, and accomplishments. However, they can also turn negative and create misalignment between here (your current level of success) and there (your desired next level of success). They can manifest into a success delusion, which is a phenomenon where you think you're a higher performer than you really are.

Similar to Marshall's success delusion, Stephen Covey's research uncovered a self-perception delusion in terms of our integrity, intent, capability, and results. Out of a possible score of one hundred, most people view their integrity at ninety-three, but when asking others to rate the perceived integrity of that person, the score is just sixty-three. When it comes to intent, we self-score at ninety-one, but others score us fifty-nine. It's no better when it comes to capability or results. Our self-scores are eighty-eight and eighty-two as compared to others scoring us at forty-four and forty-five, respectively.

This is important because our success delusion can blind us to the fact that we may not be nearly as good as we think we are, and thinking of ourselves more positively may unintentionally inhibit our motivation to learn, inhibit our ability to change, and inhibit our ability to succeed. This, in turn, can cause serious liabilities to us personally and to the teams of people whom we work with and lead. It's for this reason that we note, if you're not learning, you're in trouble.

Don't rely on your past success. Rely instead on your learning.

Rule 53. There will be good days and bad days; learn from both.

Everyone wants to be great. But I am sure we can all agree that some days are easier than others. Some days we wake up, and our hair is already perfect, our clothes look great on us, we feel great, it's a sunny seventy-five-degree day, the coffee we just brewed brings back experiences of a time in Spain when the coffee had just the right amount of richness under just the right amount of crema, the songs on our drive into the office are favorites, all the traffic lights are green in our favor, the office is abuzz with positive energy, all the work our colleagues promised would be done by today is done, our big presentation wows the investors, the dinner party that follows is just the right amount of joyous without getting out of hand, and the night is capped off with a full-bodied Meritage from Northern California as you peacefully sit at home and look at the cityscape aglow in lights and call it a day. It wasn't just a good day; it was a great day.

However, great isn't a word used to describe all our days or how we think of ourselves every day. Some days we wake up late because our phone's alarm didn't go off since the battery ran dead (stupid short-life battery!), which means we need to rush through our morning routine and miss our workout. We open a container of yogurt for a quick breakfast just to find a moldy science project has started growing inside (argh!), jump into the shower for two minutes, can't find anything good to wear and just throw on an old pair of khakis and a clean shirt, get to the platform just in time to see the train rolling away, and finally reach the office only to have a colleague point out the ripped seam in the back shoulder of the clean shirt (which could be due to excessive workouts creating bulging muscles beneath the shirt...but that would be a lie). The new product pitch we worked on all night for the big presentation today has been canceled and the product postponed indefinitely due to budget cuts. Not great! In fact, it's pretty bad.

We all have days like these. Some days are up. Some days are down. Some days it seems everything is in our favor. Other days it seems everything is working against us. Remember rule 45: *life's not fair.*

If you're human (which we're going to assume at this point!), you've experienced good days and bad days. In fact, when asked, most days fit into either of those two categories—some with immense joy and others with equally profound sorrow, some quite productive and others dogged by distraction, some faced with passionate procrastination and others with abundant enthusiasm. We don't control all the variables that make up our experiences, but some things are going to go the way we intend (or possibly even exceed expectations), and some aren't going to measure up (or will be downright lousy!). We each have limits as well as potential within each of our days.

The positive in all this is that both good days and bad days, good moments and not-so-good moments, contain lessons—things we can learn from. It's more widely practiced to learn from bad days. A team that misses project targets, an outage that lasts longer than it should, the time you made a critical error that resulted in severe consequences, the moments of crisis that shake us, or any other experienced slump—all these will often cause immediate action to reflect on what went wrong so it doesn't happen again. That's good learning and a part of good leadership. Some might say a failure is only a failure if we don't learn something from it. But we also need to learn from the good days. What made it a good day? How can we repeat that experience? How can we take what worked and make it even better?

The key to learning is to develop learning consistency and to approach each and every situation as an opportunity to learn— whether you've had a radical success, dismal failure, or something in between. Remember, go in as a learner. Leadership is not a reserved right for a select few. Leadership is a learnable set of behaviors and capabilities. It's an attitude. It's a mindset. It's a belief and determination to get better and better over time and with experience. As we learned from Regis Mulot, the chief human resource officer at Staples, "The best leaders make every day a learning experience."

There's an adjacent rule here to point out in addition to learning from good days and bad and that is to always look for opportunities to learn, but don't dwell on opportunities missed. When learning from bad days, bad moments, and bad experiences, the value is in learning and moving on. If we get stuck and dwell on the lessons of missed opportunities, we'll miss the next opportunity, which is certain to be right around the corner. So be constantly on the lookout for opportunities to learn—in both the good and the bad. Then take that learning and look for the next opportunity to apply it.

Rule 54. Look for your next best move.

The best leaders want to achieve greatness—not just for themselves but for those around them. Most often, achieving greatness will require change. Whether it's moving from individual contributor to a leader of people or from one division to another or perhaps from one company to another, from time to time, we'll need to make a move. Relative to this, a former officer at IBM talked about the need to develop an opportunistic mindset: "You've got to be prepared for almost anything and jump when opportunities happen. Have the confidence to learn quickly and grow. Learn every day and stay positive."

You know sometimes that you're the right person at the right time to lead. Other times, however, you know you need to step aside, step back, step out, or move on. Dave Estlick, a senior vice president at Starbucks, said, "If you can't be your best, get out." Similarly, Ken Avner, the senior vice president and chief financial officer at HCSC, said, "You get to the stage where you say, 'I don't know if I can take this on.' Maybe it's time to let someone else have a shot at it." That's not easy to do. This is about both life and career, and we learned about managing this from Christine Vanderpool, the chief information security officer at Molson Coors Brewing Company, who said, "First, you have to own it. Take ownership on going when you want to go. Second, create your personal mission statement. My mission statement is to be that go-to person for my leadership team when they have a problem or a question about security. Third, define who you are as a brand. Think of yourself as a product on a shelf. How am I going to get the customer to choose me instead of my competitor? Fourth, know that this isn't about career development. It's about career fulfillment." You've got to know who you are, what you want, and what you're willing to give. You've got to contribute and feel good about that. You've got to be happy, and sometimes that means making a move.

We're happiest when we're doing what we do best, and that may very well change over time. Warren Bennis, the distinguished faculty member, former university president, and prolific author, once said, "People who can't invent and reinvent themselves must be content with borrowed postures, secondhand ideas, and fitting in instead of standing out." To be your best, you've got to see a future that excites you.

Be ready for that next opportunity, and be brave enough to seize it when it presents itself to you. According to that executive we referenced earlier from the supply-chain logistics company, "You have to have your antennas up and your radar on. Know what is going on in your ecosystem and know the changes that are happening."

Be ready to make a move—that means starting with what you're doing today. We learned this from Julia Davis, the senior vice president and chief information officer at Aflac, who said, "The courage you demonstrate today shows that you're ready for your next opportunity." We've got to be ready for that opportunity. Be ready to make a move so you can be the best possible version of yourself.

Learning: Reflect, Review, and Commit

- Considering how quickly information is becoming out-dated, what's an area of your leadership where you need to devote some attention to learning? Document some deliberate ways you can go about learning to stay aligned with the moving target of leadership.

- Do you have a structured, consistent process for obtaining feedback? Take a moment to consider someone who might be able to provide you with some important feedback, and lay out a plan for how you intend to go about getting and implementing that important information.

- We all have blind spots. What are some potential ones for you? Where might your own success be working against you? What success delusions do you have? How might adopting more of a learning mindset help you see things more clearly and thus experience personal improvement?

- Think back to the last really good day (or exceptional moment or experience) you had and also a really bad day (or dismal moment or experience) that you lived. What really happened? What can you learn from that good experience in hopes of replicating it? What can you learn from that bad experience in hopes of not doing the same thing twice?

- Knowing what you know about yourself, including your strengths and the alignment between your strengths and the choices in front of you, what's your next best move? How will you maximize the future? What steps can you take that'll lead to greater personal, team, and organizational success?

Section 4: Station Break

We're successful because we do a lot right. Sometimes we do a lot right in spite of the things we need to change. Think about it. As an individual contributor at the bottom of the leadership ladder, you worked hard to prove yourself. As you move up, things change. You realize the things that made you successful as an individual contributor aren't the same things that'll make you successful as a frontline manager. And what made you successful as a frontline manager aren't the same things that'll make you successful as a middle manager. And, yep, you guessed it, what made you successful as a middle manager won't be the same things that'll make you successful as an executive. In short, your prior success is no guarantee of future success.

Success is a moving target. Therefore, your effectiveness as a leader is also a moving target. To be successful, you're going to need to change, and that means you're going to need to continually learn. The best consider continual learning to be grounded in discipline. The success you have will be realized only through persistent action, followed by reflective learning and then reaction. It's a perpetual cycle. If you're going to succeed, you're going to learn. The more disciplined learning you can create, the better. Never stop learning.

Speaking of learning, on our journey from Seattle to Chicago, you're likely rolling into your final destination by this point. Chicago has long been recognized as a world center of learning due to its institutes of higher education and research. Therefore, it's a great place to think about personal growth and development. Pause, reflect, and talk with your friends, neighbors, colleagues, and other leaders about where you are and where you're going. Spend some time to think about the five rules from section 4 and the prior forty-nine rules from the other sections. While you think about these rules, consider the following.

- Which one or two rules from this section really resonated with you the most? How do you intend to put them into practice in the near future?
- By now, you've likely developed a pretty strong vision of your intended leadership style. Realize that your style will have to evolve over time as the world and people around you change. What rules of your own are you adding into your personal leadership style to assure continual learning?

No doubt, along your journey, you've found leadership to be a process and realized it's a learning journey as much as anything else. You never really "arrive" when it comes to leadership, but now—in Chicago—we suspect that you'll leave the train, walk out of the station, and think, "Wow! What a ride."

Your success as a leader requires the strength and efficacy of a strong foundation—your mindset, purpose, and perspective—but that alone will not guarantee your success. The pillars of your leadership—your vision, preparation, and action—are necessary for you and your team to succeed. So, too, is your ability to connect with people—through people leadership, team leadership, and self-leadership. But while all that is important for success, your success won't be sustained without learning. If you can think of a great leader, you've also identified a great learner. The best leaders are the best learners. Those leaders who are truly exceptional develop themselves to be so. Leadership is learned, and the way to become great and get continually better is to learn from your experience and the experience of others. That's been the focus of this station break.

Section 5
The Conclusion of Great Leaders and Leadership

Leadership. It can make average good. It can make good great. It can engender a sense of meaning and purpose in our work. It can even transform a group of people into a high-performing team. People want truly exceptional leaders to follow. Teams need these leaders to help them navigate the changes and challenges they face every day. It's because of this that leadership matters.

The best, truest, and most authentic leaders have their leadership "built in" to who they are, not "bolted on" as an afterthought of who they should be. These leaders know that their work is a journey, and while reaching their vision and accomplishing their goals is important, their success is made possible only in how they show up every day throughout the journey, not just at their final destination. They know any leadership rule can be applied if it's convenient to do so, but it takes commitment, care, and character to live out the proven rules of effective leadership every day. The goal of this workbook is not only to outline the proven rules for effective leadership but also to demonstrate how and why to build these rules into your leadership every day.

Each rule, in part, has helped leaders we know and admire do great work and be recognized as truly exceptional. By applying the rules, collectively, we've seen existing leaders get even better and aspiring leaders get ready to be exceptional for those they lead.

Your effectiveness as a leader is determined by your ability to align your actions with intended outcomes in both good times and bad. If you've taken the time to study each rule, understand it, internalize it, and build it into your leadership style, you've no doubt already seen improved effectiveness in both life and career. Not only have you gotten better, but your teams, company, and community have likely improved as well.

You have an impact on everyone around you. Whether you know it or intend for it to happen, you do. People react to you based on how they see you and how they perceive you as a leader. It's from that perspective (their perspective) that they'll define your effectiveness and your legacy. That's why we asked these questions: What shows up when you do? What will you do with the world as you find it?

Applying the rules from this workbook—and the rules you've created from studying this workbook—can help answer those questions based on the way you lead. As we mentioned early in this journey, the important aspect of answering either of those questions is in discovering how you'll align your actions with intended outcomes so that reality plays out the way you desire. It's a process, and how you go about it is your leadership style.

The two analogies used throughout this workbook no doubt helped facilitate your understanding of what truly exceptional leadership is and how to go about it. The one analogy was used to help with the development of your leadership style; it focused on building a physical structure, which represented a way for you to think about being a leader and how to development your leadership style. The other analogy was an illustrated train ride. It was used to emphasize the process of leadership and that it's a journey.

Leadership is a process. The rules in this workbook are meant to be practiced and honed over time, because as Aristotle said, "We are what we repeatedly do. Excellence then, is not an act, but a habit." While there's no silver bullet for effective leadership, the rules are as close as you'll ever get to a formula for being a great leader. That formula starts with your foundation (section 1) of mindset, purpose, and perspective. Grounded in that foundation are the three pillars of leadership (section 2), including vision, preparation, and action. When it comes to action and leadership, it's all about people (section 3). The foundation of your leadership is core to your success, and the pillars are core to upholding what's necessary to engage people, which is contained in your capacity for people leadership, team leadership, and self-leadership. While all that's necessary to being successful at any given point in time, in order to be effective and successful over a sustained period of time, you need to learn in order to prepare for the needs of tomorrow (section 4). The four sections that make up this workbook contain rules associated with these four leadership conditions:

- The *foundation* of great leaders and leadership
- The *pillars* of great leaders and leadership
- The *people* practices of great leaders and leadership
- The *learning* practices of great leaders and leadership

You'll find yourself in these conditions at varying times in your life and career, and in many cases, you may need to work through each condition simultaneously. It's complex. It's messy. It's a work of art. And it's not in the throes of a leadership challenge that you should consider the leader you want to be. You should know that now with your rules of leadership.

Think back along your journey to this point. Think about the rules most important to you—the ones that remind you who you are and the leader you aim to be. If you were to distill those rules into a statement (or a few sentences), what would it be? Think of this as your leadership mantra, mission statement, or oath as a leader. Write it down.

_____

_____

_____

_____

_____

_____

_____

_____

_____

_____

_____

_____

_____

Read back through your leadership statement. That's your leadership oath to yourself, your team, your company, your family, and your community. There's a power in thinking about your leadership oath. That power becomes more of a guiding force when you get it out of your head and have it written down. It becomes even more powerful when you share it with others, which is what we recommend you do right now.

Take your leadership oath along with your rules and share them with others—your team, your mentor, and other friends and colleagues. Ask them to hold you accountable to the leader you aspire to be. That's what the best leaders want: to be found accountable.

You're a leader. You're accountable for what shows up when you do. You're accountable for what you will do with the world as you find it. Your rules for effective leadership and your oath as a leader will help guide your effectiveness through your journey in life and career.

APPENDIX 1: THE CANOPY OF GREAT LEADERSHIP

So there you have it: fifty-four proven rules for effective leadership as applicable in life as they are in your career. As you go about both, remember that leadership is a process. It's a journey.

You'll no doubt remember the stops along your journey from Seattle to Chicago that enabled you to focus on your mindset, purpose, and perspective, which are the foundation of your leadership. Then there was the focus on your vision, preparation, and action, which make up the three pillars of your leadership. Then there was a pause to focus on team leadership, people leadership, and self-leadership, which are the practices of your leadership taking place around the pillars and upon your foundation. Additionally, we discussed focusing on learning because leadership is always a moving target, which means that your effectiveness over time is contingent upon learning. If there's a piece missing from this journey, it's the canopy of your leadership.

The overarching canopy of great leaders and leadership is composed of four rules, and each is important to all of the prior fifty-four rules. Remember, because leadership is a process, you'll never really "arrive." But with a strong foundation and canopy, following your rules of leadership will serve to support and protect you and others as you journey.

The four rules that make up the leadership canopy include these:

Rule 55.   Be the heliotropic effect.
Rule 56.   There's power in thanks.
Rule 57.   Be kind—show compassion, forgiveness, and empathy.
Rule 58.   Enjoy the journey.

These rules are in the appendix not as an afterthought but as a means to draw even more attention to them as being necessary for everything you do and, importantly, how. Keep all fifty-eight rules in mind as you venture out on your next journey, whether your starting point is Chicago or anywhere else.

Rule 55. Be the heliotropic effect.

How well do you remember your middle school biology class? Whether you're reminiscing fondly right now about an amazing experience or starting to get a minor panic attack over the possibility of a pop quiz, we're sure you'll remember the heliotropic effect and its power and importance.

The heliotropic effect is about energy. It's easiest to understand and to (literally) see when the plant on your windowsill moves toward the sun—toward life-giving energy. That movement is the heliotropic effect (also referred to as phototropism), and its power is visible in all living things.

Like plants, people gravitate toward energy-giving sources. Think about the relationships you have. Like everyone, we suspect some people who come to mind right now drain your energy, but there are others with whom you feel great and energized. Those people are positive energizers. Like the sun to the plant on your windowsill, they're a great example of the heliotropic effect—the energizing effect they have on you.

Are you a positive energizer? Do you make everyone around you better? Do you create a heliotropic effect? An interesting example of someone who does is Shane Battier. If you're a basketball fan, you may know the name. He became known while playing at Duke University and from an NBA career spanning 2001 to 2014. His name, however, isn't among the most famous in basketball, but the reason Shane is so important is because he's an energizer.

In a *New York Times* article, Michael Lewis described Battier as "the No-Stats All-Star." It's noted in the article that "his conventional statistics are unremarkable: he doesn't score many points, snag many rebounds, block many shots, steal many balls or dish out many assists." So what makes him an all-star? Basketball insiders would point you to the "plus-minus" score, which measures the difference in the score when a player is on the court. Good players are noted to have a plus-minus score of +3. This means that while that good player is on the court, the player's team scores three more points than the opponent's team. Battier's plus-minus score is +10! When he's on the court (or on your team), he makes everyone better. He's an energizer, and it's not by accident. In a separate article, Shane noted that it's his modus operandi: "That's all I try to do. That's my mindset: I want my plus-minus to be up as high as possible. I take pride in that."

You're either life giving or life draining to those around you. We bet most, if not all, of the great leaders in your life have been positive energizers. Thinking of this conjures thoughts of the German writer Johann Wolfgang von Goethe. He wrote:

> I have come to the frightening conclusion that I am the decisive element. It is my personal approach that creates the climate. It is my daily mood that makes the weather. I possess tremendous power to make life miserable or joyous. I can be a tool of torture or an instrument of inspiration, I can humiliate or humor, hurt or heal. In all situations, it is my response that decides whether a crisis is escalated or de-escalated, and a person is humanized or de-humanized. If we treat people as they are, we make them worse. If we treat people as they ought to be, we help them become what they are capable of becoming.

The heliotropic effect is about providing the positive energy needed to allow organisms to become what they're meant to be and to enable them to reach their full potential. Be the heliotropic effect for your team, organization, and community.

Rule 56. There's power in thanks.

We learned from Cathie Brow, the senior vice president of human resources at Revera, a simple fact that often goes overlooked:

"People like to be asked and they like to be thanked." Of course we do! It makes us feel valued. It's for this reason that we mentioned in rule 9 that *the best leaders ask, listen, and thank people around them.* We're reiterating it here in a separate rule because of its importance.

Think of the last time you received a genuine thank-you. We hold the door for someone and in exchange receive a kind gesture of thanks. We pass the salt at a dinner party and receive a gracious nod. We wave someone changing lanes on a busy freeway in ahead of us and see a courteous wave and peace sign in an effort to say thanks. All that's great, but when was the last time you got a truly heartfelt thank-you for a job well done? Or, perhaps even more important, when was the last time you gave such a thank-you?

"Thank you!" is the simplest form of recognizing someone. William Shakespeare expressed the importance of giving thanks in *Twelfth Night.* You may be familiar with the play, and if so, you'll likely remember the line: "I can no other answer make, but, thanks, and thanks."

Expressions of gratitude often are given at a low cost but received with great worth. That's the kind of exchange great leaders are always looking to make. There are few ways to make someone feel more valued, validated, and recognized than telling and showing them you're grateful for them—what they accomplish, how they show up, what they contribute, what they enable, and who they are.

When people are valued, validated, and recognized, they feel as if they're an important part of the team, organization, or community, and it shows in their work and overall attitude. If you're looking for a simple way to create a heliotropic effect, this is it!

So when was the last time you really felt valued, validated, and recognized? What made you feel that way? Chances are it involved either someone asking you for your input or thanking you for your contribution. Sure, there are a variety of things that can make someone feel valued. Right at the top of the list is asking and thanking. People love to be heard and to know that their voices and opinions count. Equally, people enjoy hearing that their efforts matter and that someone else saw the value of their contributions and was pleased as a result.

Make a difference today. Ask for input. Get involvement from others by asking their opinions. Tap into the expertise and differences of others. And then provide a sincere thank-you. Write a short note of gratitude. Leave a voice mail of thanks. Or stop by, look them in the eyes, and offer a sincere thanks. Watch how people respond. They'll be glad that you asked and thanked, and so will you!

Rule 57. Be kind—show compassion, forgiveness, and empathy.

We teach a business-leadership program that includes a section on compassion, forgiveness, and empathy. We start it the same way each time, saying, "We recognize that many of you already have an advanced degree in business. We bet, however, in all of your business courses, you didn't read or study much on the need for compassion, forgiveness, or empathy." With a room full of nodding heads, we dive into the importance and power of these three actions, which can essentially be rolled up into the act of being kind.

We're always amazed that managers and leaders discover that kindness works. It does! And it should be one of the simplest things for a person to do.

Our friend Casey Woodworth documented the power of kindness as part of her leadership oath while participating in a leadership-development program. She said, "It's never the wrong choice to act with kindness, and I think in the long run it helps you get far more out of the people you manage." We agree.

It was Aesop who said, "No act of kindness, no matter how small, is ever wasted." And Plato offered this reasoning: "Be kind, for everyone you meet is fighting a harder battle."

We need more kindness in business and life. Displaying kindness can be a lever to make everything better. It's simple. It doesn't cost anything. All of us have the capacity to use it and receive it—the best leaders do so every day.

So be kind.

Rule 58. Enjoy the journey.

Often, when on a journey, we focus on the end. Rarely do we think about the planes, trains, and intermediate stops along the way; instead, we keep our eyes on the final destination. Leadership's not too terribly different. Many times we're staring at the launch date of a product or the close date of a big deal rather than the many stops and points of connection along the way. Why wouldn't we? There usually aren't big celebrations or awards given out in the middle of a journey. Those ceremonies are reserved for when the destination is reached and the goal achieved.

The best leaders, however, know the importance of the journey itself. It's the journey that's remembered. The awards, launches, and celebrations are joyous, and while plaques and trophies serve as reminders, it's the journey that's important. It's the journey and the work with others along the way that make possible the awards and launches—and yes, the celebrations.

We know Robert Hastings understands this because of the way he wrote *The Station*, from which the following is an excerpt:

Uppermost in our conscious minds is our final destination—for at a certain hour and on a given day, our train will finally pull into the station with bells ringing, flags waving, and bands playing. And once that day comes, so many wonderful dreams will come true. So restlessly, we pace the aisles and count the miles, peering ahead, waiting, waiting, waiting for the station.

"Yes, when we reach the station, that will be it!" we promise ourselves. "When we're eighteen...win that promotion...put the last kid through college...buy that 450SL Mercedes-Benz...have a nest egg for retirement!"

From that day on we will all live happily ever after.

Sooner or later, however, we must realize there is no station, no one place to arrive at once and for all. The true joy in life is the trip.

It's the trip, the journey, that matters most. While the awards and launches and celebrations are joyous, the journey is the real joy. Hunter S. Thompson, the journalist and author best known for writing *Fear and Loathing in Las Vegas*, of which we're fans, also understands this perspective. He said, "Life should not be a journey to the grave with the intention of arriving safely in a pretty and well preserved body, but rather to skid in broadside in a cloud of smoke, thoroughly used up, totally worn out, and loudly proclaiming, 'Wow! What a ride!'"

Indeed. Leadership principles stress the importance of vision, goals, and future states. But the most exciting part of being a leader is the journey you take with others—those people who follow you on that path and who enable the vision, goals, and future states to be realized.

Enjoy the journey!

APPENDIX 2: PROVEN RULES FOR EFFECTIVE LEADERSHIP

The foundation of great leaders and leadership
Mindset
Rule 1.   The foundation of success is a positive mindset.
Rule 2.   You're right about your belief in yourself.
Rule 3.   Don't confuse self-doubt with someone else's insecurity.
Rule 4.   You may not get the chance to do a better job tomorrow.

Purpose
Rule 5.   Don't forget why you do what you do.
Rule 6.   If you don't care, no one else will either.
Rule 7.   Know what you're willing to give.
Rule 8.   The purpose of business is people serving people.
Rule 9.   The purpose of people is finding meaning in work.
Rule 10.   Leadership is art, and you sign your name to it every day.

Perspective
Rule 11.   Your perspective may be yours alone.
Rule 12.   Have a point of view, but be willing to change it.
Rule 13.   Stop believing everything you think.
Rule 14.   No one has all the answers all the time.

The pillars of great leaders and leadership
Vision
Rule 15.   Greatness is never achieved while maintaining the status quo.
Rule 16.   Don't fall victim to fear disguised as practicality.
Rule 17.   Setting and realizing a vision is hard, not impossible.
Preparation
Rule 18.   Hope is not a strategy.
Rule 19.   Don't mistake a clear vision with a short distance.

Rule 20. If you're going to succeed, you've got to prioritize.

Rule 21. Small details never are.

Rule 22. Excellence is not an exception.

Action

Rule 23. Err on the side of action.

Rule 24. You don't need unanimous consent to move forward.

Rule 25. Don't confuse effort with progress or output with outcomes.

Rule 26. Don't get your actions ahead of your culture's readiness to act.

Rule 27. However bad you think it is, it's not as bad as you think.

Rule 28. Play both defense and offense.

Rule 29. Measure what matters—only what matters.

Rule 30. Don't let yesterday's frustrations hijack today's successes.

Rule 31. Did I do my absolute best today?

The people practices of great leaders and leadership

People leadership

Rule 32. Make it personal.

Rule 33. Control things, manage processes, and lead people.

Rule 34. Work with people from where they are.

Rule 35. Don't try to be a friend; rather, be a friendly leader.

Rule 36. Learn from others and pass it on.

Team leadership

Rule 37. Wearing a uniform doesn't make a team.

Rule 38. Nobody's bigger than the team.

Rule 39. Never walk past a mistake.

Rule 40. Don't confuse being right with getting it right.

Rule 41. Find a way to say yes.

Rule 42. When it comes to engagement, you won't get everyone.

Rule 43. You're not your team, but you're defined by your team.

Rule 44. Your success is a social journey.

Self-leadership
    Rule 45. Life's not fair; get used to it.
    Rule 46. You can't control your situation, but you can control your choice.
    Rule 47. You bring your weather.
    Rule 48. You can't wait to be great.
    Rule 49. You're leading and leaving a legacy; act accordingly.

The learning practices of great leaders and leadership
Learning
    Rule 50. Leadership's a moving target.
    Rule 51. Feedback accelerates learning, which accelerates greatness.
    Rule 52. If you're not learning, you're in trouble.
    Rule 53. There will be good days and bad days; learn from both.
    Rule 54. Look for your next best move.

The canopy of great leaders and leadership
Bonus rules
    Rule 55. Be the heliotropic effect.
    Rule 56. There's power in thanks.
    Rule 57. Be kind—show compassion, forgiveness, and empathy.
    Rule 58. Enjoy the journey.

ENDNOTE

Introduction

Marc Varner, "Keep a List of Life and Leadership Influencers," YouTube, October 5, 2015, https://www.youtube.com/watch?v= Gj04HbwWY04.

User Guide

National Railroad Passenger Corporation, "Empire Builder Train Route Guide," Amtrak, 2010, https://www.amtrak.com/content/dam/projects/dotcom/english/public/documents/routeguides/Amtrak-Empire-Builder-Train-Route-Guide.pdf.

Harry M. Kraemer, "How Self-Reflection Can Make You a Better Leader," KelloggInsight, December 2, 2016, https://insight.kellogg.northwestern.edu/article/how-self-reflection-can-make-you-a-better-leader.

Section 1

Nick Stockton, "Elon Musk Announces His Plans to Colonize Mars," Wired, September 27, 2016, https://www.wired.com/2016/09/elon-musk-colonize-mars/.

Colin Powell, *It Worked for Me: In Life and Leadership* (New York, NY: HarperCollins, 2012).

Ashley Ferguson, "You Need to Embrace the Idea of Change," YouTube, October 5, 2015, https://www.youtube.com/watch?v= 35nqyJOZHZU&t=1s.

Simon Cassidy, "Whether You Think You Can or Think You Can't—You're Right," Higher Education Academy, March 2015, https://www.heacademy.ac.uk/%E2%80%9Cwhether-you-think-you-can-or-you-think-you-cant-youre-right%E2%80%9D.

Suzie Smibert, "Have Trust in Yourself," YouTube, October 5, 2015, https://www.youtube.com/watch?v=MQwTFEIAihk.

Cheryl Smith, e-mail message to the authors, October 17, 2017.

Tom Schulman, *Dead Poets Society*, directed by Peter Weir, Burbank, CA: Touchstone Home Entertainment, 2006.

Jan Dean (retired executive), in discussion with one of the authors, October 2014.

Simon Sinek, *Start with Why: How Great Leaders Inspire Everyone to Take Action* (New York, NY: Penguin Group, 2009).

Simon Sinek, *Find Your Why: A Practical Guide for Discovering Purpose for You and Your Team* (New York, NY: Penguin Group, 2017).

"Quote by Friedrich Nietzsche," Goodreads, https://www.goodreads.com/quotes/137-he-who-has-a-why-to-live-for-can-bear.

Tim Callahan, "People Do Not Care What You Know until They Know That You Care," YouTube, October 15, 2015, https://www.youtube.com/watch?v=KFJTBBlnLhc&t=10s.

Dale Carnegie, *How to Win Friends and Influence People* (New York, NY: Simon and Schuster, 1937, 2015).

"H. L. Hunt Quotes," Brainyquote, https://www.brainyquote.com/quotes/quotes/h/hlhunt132394.html.

"Two Wolves," First People, http://www.firstpeople.us/FP-Html-Legends/TwoWolves-Cherokee.html.

Tom Peters and Robert Waterman, *In Search of Excellence* (New York, NY: Harper & Row, 1982).

Rosabeth Moss Kanter, *Supercorp: How Vanguard Companies Create Innovation, Profits, Growth, and Social Good* (New York, NY: Crown Business, 2009).

Stanley Weiser and Oliver Stone, *Wall Street*, directed by Oliver Stone, Twentieth Century Fox, 1987.

Dodge v. Ford Motor Co. 1991, 204 Michigan, 459, 179 N.W. 668, 3 A.L.R. 413.

Amy Messersmith, "Leadership Unboxed," https://www.evanta365.com/#/posts/11867.

PSRW, "Q&A with Dr. David A. Bray," Management Concepts, May 6, 2015, http://blogs.managementconcepts.com/psrw-qa-with-dr-david-a-bray/#.Wcw9ypOGOCU.

Gary Warzala, "Coast-to-Coast CISO Journey," https://www.evanta365.com/#/posts/11646.

Dave Estlick, "Security on Caffeine," https://www.evanta365.com/#/posts/10269.

Ryan Russell, in discussion with one of the authors, June 2016.

Cathie Brow, "Serious about Work, Fun on the Job," https://www.evanta365.com/#/posts/11100.

Colin Powell, "Why Leadership Matters in the Department of State," GovLeaders, October 28, 2003, http://govleaders.org/powell-speech.htm.

Colton Janes, e-mail message to the authors, October 23, 2017.

Veresh Sita, "Soaring into the Cloud," https://www.evanta365.com/#/posts/11911.

Daniel Goleman, *Emotional Intelligence: Why It Can Matter More Than IQ* (New York, NY: Bantam Books, 1995).

"Quote by Mark Twain," Goodreads, https://www.goodreads.com/quotes/22595-it-s-not-what-you-don-t-know-that-kills-you-it-s.

Roland Cloutier, "Do You Have a Leadership Stump Speech?" YouTube, October 5, 2015, https://www.youtube.com/watch?v=0qEMzCcP3bI.

Roland Cloutier, *Becoming a Global Chief Security Executive Officer: A How-To Guide for Next Generation Security Leaders* (Waltham, MA: Elevier, 2016).

Colleen Wood, "Appealing Deals for a New Workforce," https://www.evanta365.com/#/posts/11149.

Craig Dowden, "Words of Wisdom from the World's Top Executive Coach, Marshall Goldsmith Part 2 of 3," Financial Post, May 11, 2017, http://business.financialpost.com/executive/words-of-wisdom-from-the-worlds-top-executive-coach-marshall-goldsmith-part-2-of-3.

Marshall Goldsmith, "The Success Delusion: Why It Can Be So Hard for Successful Leaders to Change," Marshall Goldsmith, October 29, 2015, http://www.marshallgoldsmith.com/articles/the-success-delusion/.

Marc Alpert and Howard Raiffa, "A Progress Report on the Training of Probability Assessors," in *Judgment under Uncertainty: Heuristics and Biases,* Daniel Kahneman, Paul Slovic, and Amos Tversky (Cambridge University Press, 1982), 294–305.

Barry Melnkovic, "On the Right Leadership Track," https://www.evanta365.com/#/posts/11086.

Yanni Charaloambous, "Fueled to Succeed," https://www.evanta365.com/#/posts/10280.

Section 2

Ellen Johnson Sirleaf, *This Child Will Be Great: Memoir of a Remarkable Life by Africa's First Woman President* (New York, NY: HarperCollins, 2009).

Yanni Charalambous, "Fueled to Succeed."

Steven Harvey, "Banking on IT Security's Future." https://www.evanta365.com/#/posts/11129.

Wes Hargrove, "Continuous Improvement at 7-Eleven," YouTube, August 31, 2017, https://www.youtube.com/watch?v=d2wSO VtzSBA.

Gary Wimberly, "Prescribing a Transformation," https://www.evanta365.com/#/posts/10363.

Marshall Goldsmith and Mark Reiter, *What Got You Here Won't Get You There: How Successful People Become Even More Successful* (New York, NY: Hyperion, 2007).

"Quotes by Michelangelo Buonarroti," Goodreads, https://www.goodreads.com/author/quotes/182763.Michelangelo_Buonarroti.

Jim Carrey, "Commencement Speech," Maharishi University of Management, May 24, 2014, https://www.mum.edu/whats-happening/graduation-2014/full-jim-carrey-address-video-and-transcript/.

Jason Fell, "As Mark Zuckerberg Turns 30, His 10 Best Quotes As CEO," Entrepreneur.com, May 14, 2014.

John Kotter, *Leading Change* (Boston, MA: Harvard Business School Press, 1996).

Marc Varner, e-mail message to the authors, October 18, 2017.

Curt Hopkins, "Making Change: How Vanguard's CIO (John Marcante) Fosters Adaptation," Connected Futures, http://www.connectedfuturesmag.com/a/M16A16/making-change-how-vanguards-cio-fosters-adaptation/#.WeP6qJOGOqA.

"Quotes by Rudy Giuliani," Goodreads, https://www.goodreads.com/quotes/241378-change-is-not-a-destination-just-as-hope-is-not.

"Quotes by Achilochus," Goodreads, https://www.goodreads.com/quotes/387614-we-don-t-rise-to-the-level-of-our-expectations-we.

Richard Wiseman, *The Luck Factor: The Scientific Study of the Lucky Mind* (New York, NY: Hyperion, 2003).

"Louis Pasteur," Wikiquote, https://en.wikiquote.org/wiki/Louis_Pasteur.

John F. Kennedy, "Moon Speech," Space Movie Cinema, https://er.jsc.nasa.gov/seh/ricetalk.htm.

Louie Ehrlich, e-mail message to the authors, October 22, 2017.

Michael E. Porter, "What Is Strategy?" *Harvard Business Review*, 74(6) (1996): 61–78.

John Marcante, "Complexity Is the Enemy of Speed," YouTube, October 5, 2015, https://www.youtube.com/watch?v=7mFKeQUn4bk&list=PLDP0mR70fG12DN3A01xXNd9bEwoLu9CU-.

Jim Collins, *Good to Great* (New York, NY: HarperCollins Publishers, 2001).

Jim Collins, *Great by Choice* (New York, NY: HarperCollins Publishers, 2011).

Brian Engle, "The Best Leadership Advice," YouTube, October 5, 2015, https://www.youtube.com/watch?v=xpOMR2g_nbY&t=15s.

Joshua Beeman, "The Best Leadership Advice," YouTube, October 5, 2015, https://www.youtube.com/watch?v=aRPA_K-BzhE.

Richard Carlson, *Don't Sweat the Small Stuff…and It's All Small Stuff* (New York, NY: Hyperion, 1997).

"For Want of a Nail," Wikipedia, https://en.wikipedia.org/wiki/For_Want_of_a_Nail.

Harrison Barnes, "Pay Attention to the Details," LinkedIn, April 4, 2016, https://www.linkedin.com/pulse/pay-attention-details-harrison-barnes-6122704685888454656.

Joseph A. Michelli, *The New Gold Standard: 5 Leadership Principles for Creating a Legendary Customer Experience Courtesy of The Ritz-Carlton Hotel Company* (New York, NY: McGraw-Hill, 2008).

"Famous Quotes by Vince Lombardi," Vince Lombardi.com, http://www.vincelombardi.com/quotes.html.

American Society of Quality Control, "Top Reasons Customers Leave," Bizjournals, October 19, 1997, https://www.bizjournals.com/sanfrancisco/stories/1997/10/20/smallb3.html.

Bob Dethlefs, in discussion with one of the authors, October 2017.

Roland Cloutier, Do You Have a Leadership Stump Speech.

Jerry B. Harvey, *The Abilene Paradox* (New York, NY: AMACOM, 1988).

Liane Davey, "If Your Team Agrees on Everything, Working Together Is Pointless," *Harvard Business Review*, January 31, 2017, https://hbr.org/2017/01/if-your-team-agrees-on-everything-working-together-is-pointless.

Bob Behn, "Measure Outputs," *Public Management Report* 1, 10 (2004): 1–2.

Jana Kasperkevic, "How Many Burgers Has McDonald's Actually Sold?" Marketplace, May 26, 2017, https://www.marketplace.org/2017/05/26/business/ive-always-wondered/how-many-burgers-has-mcdonalds-actually-sold.

NPD Group, "Restaurant Burgers Had a Banner Year in 2014, Reports NPD," NPD, January 27, 2015, https://www.npd.com/wps/portal/npd/us/news/press-releases/2015/restaurant-burgers-had-a-banner-year-in-2014/.

Proverb Hunter, http://proverbhunter.com/quote/change-in-all-things-is-sweet/.

David S. Pottruck, *Stacking the Deck: How to Lead Breakthrough Change against Any Odds* (Hoboken, NJ: Wiley, 2015).

Alan Deutschman, "Change or Die," *FastCompany*, May 1, 2005, https://www.fastcompany.com/52717/change-or-die.

Powell, Colin. *It Worked for Me: In Life and Leadership.*

Russ Maritinelli, Jim Waddell, and Tim Rahschulte, *Program Management for Improved Business Results*, 2nd ed. (Hoboken, NJ: Wiley, 2014).

David Meer, "The ABCs of Analytics," Strategy+Business, Spring 2013, https://www.strategy-business.com/article/00150?gko=4502c.

Partha Srinivasa, "Fast-Paced CIO on the Go," https://www.evanta365.com/#/posts/10373.

Tom Schuman, "Measure What You Treasure," BizVoice, November/December 2016, http://www.bizvoicemagazine.com/media/archives/16novdec/Roundtable.pdf.

J. K. Rowling, "I Was the Biggest Failure I Knew," YouTube, June 9, 2017, https://www.youtube.com/watch?v=REXNOEoTTqs.

Alex Kendrick and Stephen Kendrick, *Facing the Giants*, directed by Alex Kendrick, Samuel Goldwyn Films Destination Films, 2006.

Quotations Page, http://www.quotationspage.com/quote/41305.html.

Marshall Goldsmith, "Questions That Make a Difference: The Daily Question Process," Marshall Goldsmith, http://www.marshallgoldsmith.com/articles/questions-that-make-a-difference-the-daily-question-process/.

Section 3

Cloutier, Roland. "Do You Have a Leadership Stump Speech?"

Amber Case, *An Illustrated Dictionary of Cyborg Anthropology*, 2013, http://cyborganthropology.com/store/.

Frederick Winslow Taylor, *The Principles of Scientific Management* (New York, NY: Harper & Brothers, 1911).

Cynthia Trudell, "Driving HR Performance," https://www.evanta365.com/#/posts/10825.

Robert Mark Kamen, *The Karate Kid.* Movie. Directed by John G. Avildsen. Production City, State: Columbia Pictures, 1984.

"Quote by Henry Boyle," Goodreads, https://www.goodreads.com/quotes/198313-the-most-important-trip-you-may-take-in-life-is.

Powell, Colin. Do You Have a Leadership Stump Speech.

Liane Davey, "Pitfalls to Avoid When You Inherit a Team," Harvard Business Review, July 6, 2015, https://hbr.org/2015/07/pitfalls-to-avoid-when-you-inherit-a-team.

Dale Carnegie, "Secrets of Success," Dale Carnegie, https://www.dalecarnegie.com/assets/1/7/Secrets_of_Success.pdf.

"Quote by Benjamin Franklin," Goodreads, https://www.goodreads.com/quotes/21262-tell-me-and-i-forget-teach-me-and-i-may.

Louie Ehrlich, e-mail message to the authors, October 22, 2017.

Sara Andrews, "Passing the CISO Challenge," https://www.evanta365.com/#/posts/11092.

Eric Mayrhofer, "Priceline's Jill Saverine Takes YPN through Ins and Outs of Professional Chang," retrieved from http://www.businessfairfield.com/july-ypn-lunch-priceline/.

Thornton May, *The New Know: Innovation Powered by Analytics* (Hoboken, NJ: Wiley, 2009).

Thornton May, "3 Lessons for Collaboration," Computerworld, August 15, 2017, https://www.computerworld.com/article/3216107/collaboration/3-lessons-for-collaboration.html.

Jeffrey E. Garten, "Jack Welch: A Role Model for Today's CEO?" Jeffrey Garten, September 9, 2001, http://jeffreygarten.com/articles/2001-09%20Jack%20Welch%20A%20Role%20Model%20for%20Todays%20CEO.pdf.

Tom Kendra, "Bo Schembechler's Legendary 'The Team' Speech Still Rings True Today in High School Football," The Muskegon

Chronicle, August 24, 2011, http://www.mlive.com/sports/muskegon/index.ssf/2011/08/bo_schembechlers_legendary_the.html.

"Quotes by George Bernard Shaw," Goodreads, https://www.goodreads.com/quotes/5520-a-life-spent-making-mistakes-is-not-only-more-honorable.

"Quotes by Mahatma Gandhi," Goodreads, https://www.goodreads.com/quotes/4793-freedom-is-not-worth-having-if-it-does-not-include.

"Quotes by Albert Einstein," Goodreads, https://www.goodreads.com/quotes/11509-anyone-who-has-never-made-a-mistake-has-never-tried.

James M. Kouzes and Barry Z. Posner, *A Leader's Legacy* (San Francisco, CA: Jossey-Bass, 2006).

John Marcante, "Diversified Approach to Leadership," https://www.evanta365.com/#/posts/12008.

Cheryl Smith, e-mail message to the authors, October 17, 2017.

Kathryn Schulz, "What Part of 'No, Totally' Don't You Understand?" *The New Yorker*, April 7, 2015, https://www.newyorker.com/books/page-turner/what-part-of-no-totally-dont-you-understand.

Valerie Bolden-Barrett, "Study: Disengaged Employees Can Cost Companies up to $550B a Year," HRdive, March 8, 2017, http://www.hrdive.com/news/study-disengaged-employees-can-cost-companies-up-to-550b-a-year/437606/.

Gallup, "Employee Engagement," Gallup, http://news.gallup.com/topic/employee_engagement.aspx.

Murphy, Tom. e-mail message to the authors, October 17, 2017..

Aon Hewitt, "2015 Trends in Global Employee Engagement," Aon Hewitt, 2015, http://www.aon.com/attachments/human-capital-consulting/2015-Trends-in-Global-Employee-Engagement-Report.pdf.

The Workplace Research Foundation, in "6 Eye-Opening Employee Engagement Statistics," Melissa Dawn Photiades, July 2, 2014, https://talentculture.com/6-eye-opening-employee-engagement-statistics/.

Kevin Kruse, "What Is Employee Engagement?" Forbes, June 22, 2012, https://www.forbes.com/sites/kevinkruse/2012/06/22/employee-engagement-what-and-why/#230ed38a7f37.

Anne Mulcahy, "Motivation," Story of Mulcahy, https://storyofmulcahy.wordpress.com/motivation/.

Michal Addady, "Study: Being Happy at Work Really Makes You More Productive," Fortune, October 29, 2015, http://fortune.com/2015/10/29/happy-productivity-work/.

Louie Ehrlich, e-mail message to the authors, October 22, 2017.

Bill Gates, "Rules Your Kids Did Not and Will Not Learn in School," Hawaii.edu, http://www2.hawaii.edu/~nreed/pub/11things.pdf. (Note: the rules were originally in the book *Dumbing Down America* by Charles Sykes.)

Victor E. Frankl, *Man's Search for Meaning: An Introduction to Logotherapy* (New York: Simon & Schuster, 1984).

Cynthia Trudell, "Driving HR Performance."

"Quote by Oscar Wilde," Goodreads, https://www.goodreads.com/quotes/19884-be-yourself-everyone-else-is-already-taken.

Linda Betz, "Empowering, Collaborative Leader," https://www.evanta365.com/#/posts/11106.

Tracey Arnish, "In Change, There Is Opportunity," https://www.evanta365.com/#/posts/11912.

Ryan Russell, in discussion with one of the authors, June 2016.

Louie Ehrlich, e-mail message to the authors, October 22, 2017.

Tom Murphy, e-mail message to the authors, October 17, 2017..

David Whyte, *The Heart Aroused: Poetry and the Preservation of the Soul in Corporate America* (New York, NY: Currency Books, 1996).

Jody Davids, "Leaving a Legacy of Leadership," YouTube, October 5, 2015, https://www.youtube.com/watch?v=wUiZ5HQLUEA& index=15&list=PLDP0mR70fG10w9MtpTleqdYWJ3OUWzmTt.

Jody Davids, *A Tale of Two Heroes* (Grove City, OH: Sean Flaharty, 2015).

Marc Varner, e-mail message to the authors, October 18, 2017.

Section 4

"Quote by Brian Herbert," http://brianherbertnovels.com/.

"Möbius Strip," Wikipedia, https://en.wikipedia.org/wiki/M% C3%B6bius_strip.

Jeff Immelt, "Leaders Must Drive Change," YouTube, June 3, 2010, https://www.youtube.com/watch?v=PHZ9i5Z8RQs.

Gregory H. Watson, "Cycles of Learning: Observations from Jack Welch," American Society for Quality, 2001, http://asq.org/ pub/sixsigma/past/vol1_issue1/cycles.html.

Samuel Arbesman, *The Half-Life of Facts: Why Everything Has an Expiration Date* (New York, NY: Penguin Group, 2012, 2013).

R. Buckminster Fuller, *The Critical Path* (New York, NY: St. Martin's Press, 1981).

Cheryl Smith, "One of My Favorite Things to Do," YouTube, October 5, 2015, https://www.youtube.com/watch?v=Ozrcn -jIFRA&index=2&list=PLDP0mR70fG10R6pi1XpC1PGB9WEg 4R8Uj.

Marshall Goldsmith, "Leaders Are Learners," The Learning Leader Show, June 8, 2016, http://learningleader.com/ episode-131-marshall-goldsmith-the-1-leadership-ceo-coach- in-the-world/.

Stephen M. R. Covey, *The Speed of Trust: The One Thing That Changes Everything* (New York, NY: Free Press, 2006).

Regis Mulot, "Bridging the Global HR Gap," https://www. evanta365.com/#/posts/11528.

Dave Estlick, "Security on Caffeine."

Ken Avner, "Reflecting on 30 Years of Financial Leadership," https://www.evanta365.com/#/posts/12199.

Warren Bennis, "Write Your Own Life," In *Learn Like a Leader: Today's Top Leaders Share Their Learning Journeys*, eds. Marshall Goldsmith, Beverly Kaye, and Ken Shelton (Boston, MA: Nicholas Brealey Publishing, 2010) 3–10.

Christine Vanderpool, "Securing and Building the Brand," https://www.evanta365.com/#/posts/12028.

Julia Davis, "Duck…and Stand Tall," https://www.evanta365.com/#/posts/10301.

Section 5

Michael Lewis, "The No-Stat All-Star," New York Times, February 13, 2009, http://www.nytimes.com/2009/02/15/magazine/15Battier-t.html?mcubz=0.

Tom Haberstroh, "Shane Battier and the Nuance of Basketball," ESPN, May 10, 2013, http://www.espn.com/blog/truehoop/miami-heat/post/_/id/17593/shane-battier-and-the-nuances-of-basketball.

"Quote by Wolfgang von Goethe," Goodreads, https://www.goodreads.com/quotes/59581-i-have-come-to-the-frightening-conclusion-that-i-am.

Cathie Brow, "Serious about Work, Fun on the Job.".

William Shakespeare and K. Elam, *Twelfth Night, or, What You Will* (London: Arden Shakespeare, 2008).

Casey Woodworth, e-mail message to the authors, October 18, 2017.

"Quote by Aesop," Goodreads, https://www.goodreads.com/quotes/16664-no-act-of-kindness-no-matter-how-small-is-ever.

"Quote by Plato," Goodreads, https://www.goodreads.com/quotes/1231-be-kind-for-everyone-you-meet-is-fighting-a-harder.

Robert Hastings, "The Station," in "It's the Journey that Counts," Ann Landers, Chicago Tribune, April 26, 1997, http://articles.chicagotribune.com/1997-04-26/news/9704260204_1_station-dear-ann-landers-train.

Hunter S. Thompson, *Fear and Loathing in Las Vegas* (New York, NY: Random House, 1971).

ABOUT THE AUTHORS

TIM RAHSCHULTE, PhD, has served for-profit and nonprofit organizations as a chief learning officer, chief content officer, and principal executive. He's currently a professor of business at George Fox University and an invited lecturer at several other universities and organizations.

RYAN HALLEY, PhD, is a professor of finance and the former chair of the department of business and economics at George Fox University. He also serves as a facilitator for Leadership Academy programs at CEB, a Gartner Company.

RUSS J. MARTINELLI is the president of the Innovation InSites group and the author of multiple books on program and project management, high-performance teams, and effective leadership. He has led both organizations and teams at Intel Corporation, Loral, and Lockheed Martin.

INDEX